# Sea of Voices, Isle of Story

edited by
Celeste Mergens & Marian Blue

# Sea of Voices, Isle of Story

edited by
Celeste Mergens and Marian Blue

TripleTree Publishing
Eugene, Oregon

© 2003 TripleTree Publishing

Sea of Voices, Isle of Story
A WIWA Anthology of the Best Contemporary Writing

ISBN: 0-9716638-4-X
Library of Congress number: 2002109711

TripleTree Publishing
PO Box 5684, Eugene, OR 97405
(541) 338-3184 – www.TripleTreePub.com

Cover and interior design by Alan M. Clark
Cover photo by Larry Bullis
Printed in the United States of America
1 2 3 4 5 6 7 8 9

## Dedication

To all the writers who have kept writing through indifference, poverty, and persecution to make the world a better place by telling their stories—our stories.

Royalties from the sale of this book benefit the many programs and scholarships offered by The Whidbey Island Writers Association.

# Table of Contents

**Forewords** by Marian Blue and Celeste Mergens — 10
**Firewood** by Marjiann Moss — 16
**Trees of His Own** by Antoinette Grove — 20
**Watching the Ancestral Prayers of Venerable Others**
        by Pattiann Rogers — 27
**Spade** by Maureen McGregor Scully — 29
**Instructions to a Painter** by Donald Hall — 34
**The Icehouse** by Patrick Riley — 35
**Cop School** by Helen L. Campbell — 40
**The Spray and the Slamming Sea** by Paul Lindholdt — 44
**Litany** by Diane Averill — 53
**The Flooded Forest** by Nnedi Okorafor — 54
**A Tale of Two Livers** by Ann Adams — 62
**The Narrative Thread** by Andrena Zawinski — 68
**Husbandry** by Kyle Kuhn — 70
**The Blue Butterflies** by Maurya Simon — 80
**Split Second** by Manju Kak — 81
**Fishstalker** by Ivon B. Blum — 85
**Improvements** by Patricia Brodie — 92
**A Stump Ranch Chronicle** by Rae Ellen Lee — 94
**December** by Jay Paul — 98
**Into the Box** by Kristin King — 100
**Strange Songs Beautifully** by Robin Reynolds Barre — 104
**Hallmark Cards** by JoAnn Kane — 105
**Song for a Ghost of Lake Drummond**
        by Renée Olander — 114
**Voyage of Discovery** by Barbara Whitby — 116
**Crossing Cold Water: Voyages to the Last Frontier**
        by Rebecca Goodrich — 122

**On Rain** by Susan Zwinger — 129

**The Men You Don't Get to Sleep With** by Susan Rich — 130

**Uncle Fred and the Sound of One Hand Clapping**
        by Wayne Ude — 132

**Bronco Buster** by Erv Bobo — 137

**Battlefield** by Ann Gerike — 145

**Gardening with a Pen** by Eva Shaw — 146

**With a Little Help from Raven** by Duane Niatum — 150

**Fin de Siècle Sonnet Out of Town** by Richard Robbins — 155

**Laying Down One's Life** by Christin Chaya — 156

**Goya's Monsters** by Norton Girault — 159

**Down at The Igloo** by Brian Ames — 161

**Lost Puzzle Piece** by Ron Hughes — 166

**In Love with Bobby** by Sharon Goldner — 168

**What the Blind Girl Saw** by Douglas Knox — 176

**Fog** by Kelli Russell Agodon — 180

**Getting the Message** by Elizabeth Engstrom — 181

**Obi's Catapult** by Chika Unigwe — 185

**Back to Country with Pulitzer** by Liam Rector — 190

**In Hemingway Country** by Philip Raisor — 193

**New Roads** by Natalie Olsen — 199

**Mrs. Ryan's Last Lesson** by Dorothy Read — 200

**Wolf Love** by Victory Lee Schouten — 207

**Things That Go Bump in the Lake**
        by Rowena Williamson — 208

**King of the Butterflies** by Christopher Howell — 217

**The Contributors** — 220

**About the Whidbey Island Writers Conference** — 231

# Introductions

Every year thousands of publications—magazines, books, newspapers—receive tens of thousands of stories, millions of words, from writers. Some stories are shaped as essay, some as fiction, some as poetry—but each writer seeks the story that will ground us, that will lead (or push) us, that will provide an essential truth or kernel of understanding.

Writers who have worked to create and shape these stories gnash their teeth at rejections, become despondent, rant against the publishing system. Then they write some more. Others never submit, but they keep writing.

Why do they keep telling these stories? Why do we keep reading them?

Perhaps we've never needed our stories more than we do today. People turn to story when afraid, when joyful, when confused. For instance, after terrorist attacks (9/11) on the US east coast, people felt compelled to tell their stories about heroism, about fear, about people caring for one another. We most need stories that connect events, that help us heal grief, that weave together the human family, that celebrate the beauty of humanity, that expose the parts of humanity that aren't beautiful. These stories most often remind us that the human family shares more, has more in common, than any differences that reside on the surface within particular descriptions of religion, race, age, gender or nationality; such stories bring us together during times when people with political or personal agendas would use fear or anger to drive us apart, would highlight differences rather than our similarities.

When we first discussed compiling this anthology, it was

in connection with celebrating the fifth anniversary of the Whidbey Island Writers' Conference. Immediately people wanted us to box the idea into a "theme" that would sell the book, that would give focus to the text, that would give aid to writers who had to decide what to submit; anthologies with specialized themes—some as extreme as Left-handed Duplex Dwellers of South Bend, Indiana—abound. Our question was: what theme accurately expresses our conference, which celebrates writing without boxes, without limitations. The annual Whidbey Island Writers Conference includes students and professionals; script writing, poetry, essay, articles, fiction; within those broad genres, we include literary, romance, children's, mystery, nature writing—

Diversity.

That was our theme. Not diversity in the politically correct sense of a certain percentage of male/female, a certain percentage of this ethnic group or this particular genre—such is a system one might use to produce Anatomically-Correct-Diversity.

Rather you hold in your hands an anthology that steps off the mainland of literary tradition and journeys beyond the safety of known waters. Here you will find poetry, essay and fiction; you will find romance and humor and mystery and literary and magical realist stories. You will find the voices of writers new in the work or young in years and writers who have proven themselves, have received prestigious awards in their chosen genres; you will find voices from different countries, from different belief systems. But they share their human family's concerns with peace, with aging, with the environment and human interactions with animals, with love in all relationships; all these concerns blossom into one reason why writers write and why readers read: to tell our story, to learn our story, to continue our story.

When we sent out our invitation to submit to this anthology, the material flooded in from, literally, every English-speaking country in the world and from a few where English is not the primary language. Some stories came from writers steeped in the academic traditions of writing; others have had no formal training.

In the process of reading all these submissions, I was blessed by renewing many friendships and by making some new friendships. But I was also blessed by reading the wealth of material that records our stories; I felt refreshed and enthused about our human family.

Setting aside theme, genre, and reputation of the writers, these stories, poems, and essays welcome the readers into the concerns of our global village of writers. This sea of voices symbolize the ocean of today's writers and writing. Consequently, you cannot read one piece in this anthology and assume that you know the tone, theme or style of any other piece any more than you can dive in a kelp forest and learn about a coral reef; although these voices do all meld into the harmony of "story," and they each retain the power and dignity of the individual writer's voice, each is distinct and each would normally market to a different sort of publication.

At the same time, the anthology cannot claim to contain samples of *all* the voices, styles, points of view, or genres— that would be impossible. But perhaps the variety here will lure readers to journey beyond habit, to launch themselves beyond the known waters of a favorite genre or author, and to take a voyage to discover new voices in the world's sea of writing.

The only sad aspect of editing the anthology for me is that the volume of this flood, this tsunami of submissions, meant that we had to reject wonderful writing that deserved to be included. To provide variety, we sometimes had to pick one story out of a dozen with similar themes (such as caring for the elderly or involving young people with rivers); we also decided to take no more than one piece per author, which sometimes resulted in mental wrestling among the editors who had to choose between several wonderful pieces; sometimes we had to choose according to length in order to include as many voices as possible; sometimes the decision came down to each editor releasing certain stories and accepting others that would not have not been included with a single editor—thus the voices here appear in part because of the diversity within the editors' personal visions—an aspect of diversity I had not anticipated when we began this work. All these decisions involve give and take, involve recognizing that differences are what ultimately provide the best texture of a work, of an ocean, of a life.

Ultimately, several excellent anthologies could have been woven out of the wonderful work submitted to *Sea of Voices, Isle of Story*; I look forward to the day when we have a chance to do another such anthology. Meanwhile, I'm grateful that many magazines and books are daily providing us with story, with diversity of a sort that proves how related we all are.

At no time can cultures navigate unknown seas without story tellers, without those who capture grief, humor, and wild imagination into a context we can understand. From the time of gathering around the fire to one in which we stare into the sparking light of our computer screens far into the night, our islands of story provide safe harbors, places to gather and to find psychic rest, to understand the meaning of being human.

Welcome into this circle of light. May you find the story that unlocks one of your mysteries; may you discover a new mystery to take its place and give you something to pursue for a time; may you meet a new voice that becomes a lifelong friend; may you re-discover a friend (perhaps yourself) within these pages; may you discover the healing connections within our global family's diversity; may you always enjoy celebrating the art of writing and the art of reading.

—Marian Blue

⸺•⊱⸺

Words saved my life.

Not figuratively nor in tabloid overstatement, but simply in truth, words saved my life. I learned the magic of symbols creating word paintings (story) at an early age and I swirled those "paints" into my life and found reasons for laughter, answers to questions, inspiration for creativity and hope for the future.

I read by flashlight under the blankets while shouts echoed around the house. Books brought escape, humor, adventure, and assurance that there were many, many possibilities available to me. Later, when the darkest years came it was only journaling, scripture, and uplifting literature that lent me the courage to persevere and pass through unscathed.

Writing, in any form, is a powerful thing. History is strewn with times when reading and writing were reserved for only a few or actually forbidden to the impoverished or captive in hopes of restraining them from arising.

Writing transports us to an open fount and even provides the cup from which we can drink while we refresh our spirits and gather strength and resources to continue our own journeys.

Today, I dedicate a large part of my life to supporting those who have the courage to reach within themselves and transform their thoughts, passions and perspectives into vibrant word worlds... books, poems, stories, essays, scripts, and songs. All of it is of equal importance to me. Imagine my delight when I was offered the opportunity to be part of the editorial team of an international anthology that would span many styles, many genres, many voices, as does the Whidbey Island Writers Conference whose 5th Anniversary it celebrates.

*Sea of Voices; Isle of Story* received an avalanche of outstanding contributions from around the world: some flawless, some textured in creative ways, some flowing and even some that bore tiny slumps in form and yet captured our imaginations. Hundreds of enthusiastic writers trusted us with their manuscripts, sending us into panic at being able to read them all in time. To be honest there was a moment that we actually hoped that a chunk of them would have glaring weaknesses and be easy to dismiss; only in that did they disappoint us. The submissions were a treat to revel in. And unless we had been creating a book the size of *War and Peace* we had just been given a very difficult task... selecting only a few!

The entries made us laugh, cry, sigh, groan and gasp. And when it was all said and done we wrestled over our final selections and it came down to this: those selected drew us in, introduced us to new vision, knowledge and experience, left us changed people, because for a brief moment we were in the writer's world.

And though we will not presume to say what these pages will do for you, we do hope that you will find some gift within them as you visit the places, experiences, and perspectives this anthology contains. It has been a joy bringing it to you, and I only wish that I could be there with you when you curl up with your favorite selections. Feel free to e-mail me and tell my your favorites... I may even tell you mine! You can reach me through the Whidbey Island Writers' Conference website at www.whidbey.com/writers.

May life lend you many stories, many moments to savor the flavors of diversity that our world offers and the courage to share them. And should there come a moment when you need a life preserver as I did, may you too find the perfect words to be close at hand.

Fondly,
Celeste Mergens

# Firewood

*Marjiann Moss*

We landed on the island in early October. Handwritten directions led to a faded shell of a house, listing toward Saratoga Passage. I took in the gray, watery landscape and held my baby daughter close, shivering.

Inside the cottage it was the same temperature as out. Fresh air breezed through gaps in the cedar walls, which exhaled a woodsy aroma, comforting, if not exactly warm.

"It's okay to burn driftwood," the owner had said. "Some say the salt will eat the stove, but I think that'll probably take awhile. There's some wood in the basement. Just replace what you use."

The cast-iron stove was already well ventilated, with cracks and unglazed seams breathing air like the house. Downstairs I found a paltry stack of dry wood leaning against a dirt wall - maybe enough for six weeks, if I was careful, or perhaps a winter's worth of dry kindling.

Although the beach was only fifty feet down, I was winded the first time I descended the sloping trail. Somewhere between the filing and the final decree, I had choked on the loss of my marriage. Whether I was trying to expel a clot of failure, or had merely choked on the word divorce, I had coughed ceaselessly for four months. Now, two cracked ribs later, it still took an effort to simply breathe without succumbing to the cough reflex.

I dug a broken limb of driftwood out of the sand, waterlogged and heavy as stone, but small enough to fit into the stove. Laboring up the bluff with it, I had to stop twice to rest.

"Great," I thought. "I can't carry a single piece of wood a hundred feet. How am I supposed to keep us from freezing to death all winter?"

In the following weeks my lungs and legs strengthened until I could carry two or three chunks at a time up the trail and make three or four trips at a go. I learned the meaning of "burning wood heats you twice." Only in my case, it was more like four or five times.

Even as the pile grew to something that might last through winter, if I continued gathering as I had been, I realized that this wood would not keep us warm. My fires lay there steaming and smoldering, the wood so wet the precious cedar kindling and costly chopped-up Presto Logs only caused it to sweat and simmer.

The world chilled, turning a million shades of gray. I sat at the window for hours, staring out, as if I could internalize the steel in the landscape into my bones, into my will, giving me the strength to push on. I thought of the island's earliest residents, who had lived in tents along the shore, possibly on this very bluff; most likely they had even been barefoot year-round. Then there was my great-grandmother. She had homesteaded in the Badlands, on her own—a single mother—through bitter, unforgiving winters. She had made it; so could I.

Next door, the old man had been watching my ineffectual attempts at fuel gathering. More than once, feeling eyes on me, I had glanced up to see binoculars at his window, trained down on me. He must have laughed at first at what were obviously ignorant and misdirected efforts, persistent but futile.

He had taken to following me down to the beach, toting an immense Stihl chainsaw over his shoulder for cutting up logs. Over on his hundred feet of sand, he would wade out a bit, lasso a log, and coax it in with the waves until he could balance it on chunks of wood almost clear of the water. Then he retreated to the bulkhead and split rounds until the tide had receded and the log was left high and dry. At that point he would give a yank on the Stihl and slice the log into even lengths as if it were a gigantic salami.

But no matter how he smiled and nodded and did each step of his pattern with exaggerated movements, demonstrating how well his system worked, it had no effect on my own methods. No saw. No rubber boots. I continued bending over, picking up, and tossing unpromising chunks of flotsam over the bulkhead, turning purple from the effort.

"That stuff'll never burn," he finally advised one day. "You need to get yourself a saw. Look."

He showed me a wedge of split log as though I'd never seen one, pointing out how dry and burnable it was inside. I flushed even deeper. When our eyes met, I tried to convey wordlessly that, contrary to appearances, I was not a complete idiot as far as heating with wood was concerned, and I was doing the best I could, considering.

That afternoon he knocked on my door. When he showed me an ad for a 10-inch Homelite chainsaw, the tears I had quickly snuffed to answer the door came back in force.

"If I had that kind of money, which I don't, I'd be buying cordwood with it, not a tool I can't even use!" I wailed. My fears tumbled out: of wintering in this skeletal house, the coming cold, of not being able to keep my baby safe and warm.

"Look," he encouraged. "If you buy the saw instead of wood, you can cut all the cords you want. I'll show you."

He reached into his wallet and extracted $150. "It's a loan. Pay me back when you can. No hurry." He was gone before I could say no.

Who was this stranger, who had just inserted himself into our desperate situation? I couldn't afford much contemplation; our circumstances allowed no margin for pride. I headed for town.

Back on the beach, chainsaw in hand, I discovered the relative density of cedar and fir and hemlock and also that madrona could just about burn up the chainsaw before I could cut through it. I carried a whiskbroom in my back pocket to clean the logs of debris, and soon could slice one up without dipping the saw blade into the sand. My brother-in-law, a forester, showed me the finer points of sharpening, and every night I tended that saw, filing each and every tooth at a perfect angle, and cleaning the whole machine inside and out.

We survived that first winter, if barely. The next spring my daughter's chatter from her swaddled nest on the bulkhead was drowned out by whining chainsaws as we gathered firewood, side by side with our neighbor, for the next winter to come.

# Trees of His Own

*Antoinette Grove*

For Niko the roses were the first sign if he had still believed in signs. When he was a boy his mother had pulled him out under the wide Arizona night and pointed to the stars. "See that one?" she had asked him, her finger trailing a smear of light, quickly extinguished. "It's fallin' out of the sky like it's been shot. Something bad's gonna happen now. Just you wait." And sure enough, in a week or a month, someone down in town died from taking bad meat or fell off a horse along a dry wash and was laid up for a season or two. His mother hadn't cared that the people who died were usually old and the people who fell off their horses were usually drunk. It still had been a sign.

He pulled off his worn work gloves and folded them into his back pocket, pushed the cedar bark mulch aside with the toe of his boot and bent low to rub the dark soil between his fingers. A rich layer of coffee grounds and humus promised an abundance of new, waxy green growth. Instead, the rose's foliage draped limp and curled in defeat and in some places was as dry and brittle as scorched paper.

He scanned the row of climbers along the trellised porch. Those at the opposite end already were arching and bowing their long shoots onto the gravel path. They would need to be pruned and trained upwards if they were to make half the showing they had last season. It was just the single rose bush at his end that looked parched and frail, nearest the steps and in the lee of the stout, pine hand rail. He reached for his shovel and with three quick cuts into the earth, neatly excised the rosebush from the hedge.

"Am I paying you to butcher the roses, Mr. Sanchez?"

"No, Missus," he answered without looking up from his task. He didn't need to. He could imagine her standing above him, a reprise of a thousand other mornings, coffee cup in hand, her clever eyes shaded by the brim of her straw hat, red lacquered nails drumming the porch railing like a telegraph operator, feet bare in all weather, like a peon.

This was how Mrs. Dahl greeted each morning.

She handed him down his coffee—cream, no sugar—and settled in to watch him work. For the first fifteen years, during summers and on holidays at the lake with her husband and three children, and through the last ten years as a widow living full time in the cottage alone, this is how the day began for them both.

"You been dumping the coffee grounds out here on the roots like I told you?" Niko asked her.

He leaned on his shovel and looked into her pale gray eyes. It was her eyes that always reminded him he was so far away from home, her eyes and the tall trees. As a child he would never have been able to imagine trees so plentiful, so close together the coolness of their shade was permanent. He'd warned himself a hundred times to be careful not to get lost, lost in the impenetrable trees—or her eyes.

"Of course, Mr. Sanchez. I put the grounds on the roots every morning. Just as you advised. You can see that, can't you?"

He could see that. But this bush also looked boiled as if she had one morning poured a pot of hot coffee over the leaves instead of the cooled grounds. Then, as they spoke, the way her normally direct gaze skittered away from his was the second sign. He could hear his mother's voice, see her finger mark the meteor's decent like a sure path to tragedy, yet he told himself not to worry; they weren't his roses. He told himself he only worked for the Missus. He told himself, on the way to dump the dead rosebush into the back of his beat-up Chevy pick-up, you can only borrow so much trouble, you don't have to own it.

He'd started out as summer help, someone to haul out

the lawn furniture and cut the grass before Memorial Day, see to the dock and keep the little rowboat seaworthy and tied fast. Then after Labor Day, when the city families deserted their cottages like a migrating herd, he would haul it all back and set things to right for the moths and mice until another summer when the sun slanted over the lake like a promise.

Now the children were grown and Mr. Dahl buried in the city in a grave that, Niko suspected, hadn't seen flowers since the first petals fell on his headstone ten years before. Niko imagined the city a more fitting place for Mr. Dahl, even dead and buried. The trees and sweet air had seemed to confound him, and he always had appeared to Niko to have one foot poised for a quick escape from the twin dangers of rest and relaxation.

The children, two boys and a girl, had thrived in the summer sun. Niko had taught one and then the others to swim in the dark waters beyond the dock, to dive for crawfish, to not be afraid of the looming hulks of sunken logs, to be wary of snags. Mrs. Dahl could not swim, and Mr. Dahl could not be bothered. They called him Niko. Only the Missus called him Mr. Sanchez and brought him his lunch on a china plate.

But always, after a few weeks, even the children tired of the lake, the frogs haunting its margins and the secret coves beneath leaning alders and willows. By Labor Day, neighborhood friends and school renewed their attraction. Only Mrs. Dahl glanced back, admonished him to look after the roses, and waved as their station wagon pulled off through the cedars and Douglas firs.

When her husband had died she returned to the cottage and never left. She found a rhythm and spent her days in quiet retreat, summers in the sun with a book or in the little boat on the lake teasing rainbow trout onto her line. Winters she was a contented bear, holed up during the short days and long nights, counting the birds at the feeders like a census-taker. Sometimes the children came from their jobs in the city, brought their friends, then their lovers, then their own families, but they never heard the whisper over the water or saw the trees the way Mrs. Dahl did. This Niko knew because he'd watched her for twenty-five years. He wasn't blinded, as they were, by belonging.

He had always spent his winters down south near Las Vegas doing for other families what he did for the Dahl's, but eventually he found a place to park his trailer year round in the little northern Washington town above the lake and looked for work to keep him settled and wool shirts and thick boots to keep him warm. The suburbs had crawled out from the city like a stain, and there were lawns and weeds enough to keep a man busy for fifty miles around. It was as good a time as any to root himself to one spot. In time he even set some money aside. Evenings he watched the stars; mornings were Mrs. Dahl's.

One morning after removing the dying rose bush, he came early to the cottage on the lake, drove through the misty fingers rising like ghosts from the water and found her, as he'd feared, pouring the steaming water from the glass coffee carafe over the hole where the rose bush had been. It was only water—she'd forgotten to add the grounds—but damning enough. When he tried to take it from her she called him Frank, her dead husband's name, and began to weep. Was this the third sign, he asked himself, or the hundred and third?

He remembered her odd little questions and inappropriate responses and the times when he was loathe to leave her alone. She could forget a name, a date or even a face and just be getting old. He had wrestled so long with his suspicions he'd stopped looking at the night sky for fear of seeing a meteor shower and had stumbled instead into a massive crater looming just beyond his field of vision.

He gently led her back indoors and sat her down at her kitchen table. "I'll make us some coffee and we can talk. Okay, Missus?" She nodded and wiped her nose with a cloth napkin she took from a ring at the table. There were no paper napkins, such as Niko used in his little trailer, and the table was set neatly for one with matching dishes and silverware, but for a white plastic spoon where a silver one might have rested. Had she tossed her silver spoons, like breadcrumbs, to the coots on the lake? So many pretty things here, he thought as he sought out the coffee and filters, so clean and feminine. He was a stranger here and his large, rough hands dwarfed the pair of china cups he brought to the table. Mrs. Dahl had dried her eyes but they remained luminous in a once-beautiful face whose lines showed him more character than age.

"Maybe we should talk later," Niko began. There was both fear and hope in those gray eyes. "You should rest, maybe?" He tried to rise but she placed her hand over his and pinned him with her gaze.

"We need to talk now, Mr. Sanchez, while I still can."

He settled back into his chair. Her hand remained over his. It was cool and soft and twenty-five years late. "You've seen a doctor?"

"I've seen two, in fact. They both said the same thing. My mind is going a little at a time, day by day. Unfortunately, it's not taking my body along with it for the ride. In other words," she said with a trace of a smile, "in a very few months the lights will be on but no one will be home."

He felt as if he were falling though he remained perfectly still, his boots on the floor, his hand on the table. "The children? They know?"

"No, they do not know, Mr. Sanchez, and I don't intend for them to know. They have good lives, they're happy. Why should I drag them into this?"

"They love you, Missus. They'll want to take care of you." Then, capping his argument, "Besides, how are you going to keep it from them when they come up here to visit? How you gonna keep them from knowing?" He thought of the missing spoons, the dying roses.

"Simple, Mr. Sanchez." She patted the back of his hand. "I won't be here."

He landed hard.

When he had been a small boy his world was small: four bare walls with a tin roof and his mother feeding kindling into an iron stove. He was a thousand miles and a lifetime away from that shack, but his world was again very small. He turned his hand and their fingers entwined.

They met on the dock that night, backlit by a gibbous moon. Only a handful of the dozen or so houses on the lake were lived in year round and of those only two, at the opposite end of the lake, showed light in their windows. He pulled his collar up against the half-hearted breeze and, as her flashlight bobbed nearer, he noticed she wore a fur-lined parka and over-large, rubber boots.

Without a word he helped her into the rowboat but when he made to join her she said, "I need to do this myself." The job of fitting the oars into the oarlocks escaped her, though, and in the end he climbed in, slid them home and began to row grimly out onto the lake. He had agreed to stand on shore, to see she accomplished her goal of "accidentally" drowning and then to call nine-one-one in the morning as if he were ignorant, as if he were only the gardener come to work and found his employer missing. But now he was as much a part of it as she was.

Thirty yards out he pulled in the oars. "It's a nice night," he said. "We can go back. No one will know you thought of doing this." Owls called across the water, "Whoo, whoo." *Who are you trying to save?*

"I have to do it *now*, while I'm still me, while I still know what I'm leaving." He could not see her tears but he heard them in her voice. "If I wait too long I won't be able to say goodbye. And I have to be able to say goodbye. There's too much I haven't said over the years, isn't there?" Then, with a soft whisper almost stolen in the breeze, "Frank would never have done this for me." She pushed quickly up onto the gunwale and splashed over the side.

She sank for a moment and then, despite her soggy coat and boots full of water, bobbed back to the surface in a maelstrom of flailing and sputtering. Was it confusion or the primal instinct to fight death that drove her back to the boat? "Help me!" she cried. He didn't think as he lunged forward, caught her hand and yanked her towards him. With a surprising strength she pulled free. "No! Niko, help me."

He looked at the stars. Tears blurred his vision, and they all seemed to streak through the sky.

"Help me, Niko."

He carefully climbed over the side of the rowboat, slid into the lake and felt the chill of late May move up his body in a wave until only his head and one arm on the gunwale were above the water line. His boots were heavy as anchors pulling him to the bottom, and he was thankful he would not have to depend upon his own strength to carry this through.

"Take care of the roses," she said.

"I don't work for you no more." He pulled her to him, and she pressed her head to his shoulder. "Breathe out," he told her, and when he felt her chest contract he let go of the rowboat. They embraced and, as they drifted down into darkness, she made fists against his back—open then closed—and was still. He held her, as he'd never done in life, touched her hair, brought her fingers to his lips, to his heart, then let her go.

Niko reached for the laces of his boots, untied them and kicked them free. He sped to the surface as if drawn on a string to the stars. The shore wasn't far for a good swimmer, but he wavered and looked back once before taking the first stroke. In the morning he would call the sheriff, he would lie to the children, and he would tend to the roses. Then he would take a last, long look at the trees, the constant trees.

A man could get lost in those trees.

# Watching the Ancestral Prayers of Venerable Others

*Pattiann Rogers*

Lena Higgins, 92, breastless,
blind, chewing her gums by the window,
is old, but the Great Comet of 1843

is much older than that. Dry land
tortoises with their elephantine
feet are often very old, but giant

sequoias of the western Sierras
are generations older than that.
The first prayer rattle, made

on the savannah of seeds and bones
strung together, is old, but the first
winged cockroach to appear on earth

is hundreds of millions of years
older than that. A flowering plant
fossil or a mollusk fossil in limy

shale is old. Stony meteorites buried
beneath polar ice are older than that,
and death itself is very, very

ancient, but life is certainly older
than death. Shadows and silhouettes
created by primordial seastorms

erupting in crests high above
one another occurred eons ago,
but the sun and its flaring eruptions

existed long before they did. Light
from the most distant known quasar
seen at this moment tonight is old

(should light be said to exist
in time), but the moment witnessed
just previous is older than that.

The compact, pea-drop power
of the initial, beginning nothing
is surely oldest, but then the intention,

with its integrity, must have come
before and thus is obviously
older than that. Amen.

# Spade

*Maureen McGregor Scully*

The river man had come up out of the waters sputtering and coughing and reaching out hard with his lungs for the sweet salvation of air—air, free and clean, in and out, living air. They handed him a spade and a grey uniform with a number printed on it in blue just under the words Angola State Prison.

That was the beginning, and the beginning was the word, and the word was *spade*—the spade became his pal. He put his foot to it in the corner of the exercise yard, turning up the earth. He could smell the air in it, the air, free and clean, in and out. Beneath the hard crust of the earth, he could taste the muddy waters in his nose, and this was a part of it too— earth: muddy immersion—and air, free and clean.

In the beginning the pilgrims came, the women with their faces heaped up with sadness and their bodies scrubbed into their best clothes as if their visit was an occasion, a prayer meeting. Sometimes they cried and wrung their hands and called out "Lord have mercy, Lord have mercy." Other times they reached into their pockets for candy smiles and told him stories with artificial color and flavoring. Their eyes were pole hooks stabbing at him, prodding him, trying to pull *it* out of him. But he didn't know what *it* was, knew only that they wanted something from him, something he would have surely given if he had had it or known it. Most times they brought him tasty tidbits from their kitchens or drawings from their children. He had no taste for their food but thanked them politely, and when they'd gone, he'd given the food to the other men who clamored like children for it.

He had anticipated these women first with eagerness, then with dread, and finally not at all. They were connected to the man that lay at the bottom of the muddy river, not to the man that sat before them stretching out his lungs for air. They seemed to congeal in front of him, until after awhile he could not tell one from another, could not call any face by name, could really only say the names into the air. It was only the music of their names that he could bring inside himself. He held the names there like photographs of strangers and grabbed hold of the ache because it was sweet and maybe once had been beautiful.

His first job after being born again was on the road crew, spading out sand and sometimes asphalt, spading out dirt for the culverts. Seemed like every day from first sun to first dark, he had the smooth round wood in his hands—cypress— wasn't that the holy wood? He didn't know much about holiness, though he thought he should. He knew that the man lying at the bottom of the river had been raised up by the Bible, but he couldn't reach into that man's memory now and pull anything out. If holiness was a feeling, then maybe that was the name he put to how he felt spading up earth in the exercise yard and planting apple and orange seeds from his supper.

Some of them seeds grew up, too, pushing little green heads and arms out of the brown womb, stretching out for the air and the sun, but they never lasted. They cringed under the weight of running boots, withered when angry hands ripped them from the brown breast. When he found them brown and dry, a sweet ache bounced against his ribs like an echo.

The women stopped coming months, maybe years, after he stopped anticipating them. He did receive a brown paper package one day, perhaps from one of the women. Inside were a few thorny stems and wispy roots knotted up in rich brown earth. He smiled from a place deep enough perhaps to reach the man lying at the bottom of the river. When his exercise time came, he took his spade to the corner of the yard, turned the earth anew, spaded in deep, and planted the rose. He sat the rose into the hole, gently spreading the wispy threads, seating them in the soil, and sang the name *Emmaline* –one of those sweet-remembered names—silently like an incantation. Then he mounded up the dark earth against the thorny stems, breathed in the earth's muddy fragrance. *Emmaline, Emmaline, Emmaline.*

The rose did not succumb to the hapless steps of antsy muscles in grey uniforms, nor would she permit angry hands to touch her naked flesh. So when the spring came, the leaves came too, bright and tender, like a cooing child. *Emmaline, Emmaline, Emmaline.* The new men with animals in their throats and poison on their tongues kept their distance, and the old men with eyes full of sky would squat next to her and smoke their cigarettes.

He earned four cents an hour for his labors on the road crew. Every couple of years, he'd saved enough up to buy another rose from the mail order catalog. Each rose was a different song, each song a name of a brown-faced woman, a woman that had visited perhaps, or a name that fell from the lips of the man at the bottom of the river. *Raynelle, Maretha, Shannalee, Donisha.*

He had developed a reputation now of being a good man with a spade, and when the gravedigger died (a murder one lifer named Grounder), the bootjacks with the rifles handed him the job. Sometimes in the middle of the night, they'd rattle something up against the bars, and he'd open his eyes, but he wouldn't stir. "Hey Spade," they'd say, "got a rose for you to plant." They'd laugh and mumble nonsense to themselves and walk on down the cellblock.

As the years passed, he buried a lot of men—young men eager to get it over with—old men who just laid down in it—'lectric chair men, whose death was a spectacle conjuring up salve for scabby wounds. Buried them all at night, just him and the spade and the Coleman lantern and a bootjack with a rifle and an attitude. The burying place was rocky, and sometimes the spade would ring against a rock, peal like a bell in someone else's ear, sounds in the ear of the man at the bottom of the river.

Some guy in a preacher collar gave him a Bible—and for a long a time it just leveled out the legs of his chair so it didn't rock when he sat in it. But after a while he took to reading it, maybe because he was curious, maybe because the thought fell out of the river man's head and floated up to the surface where he could scoop it up and taste it. Whatever the reasons, he read it and liked the stories and language and what it had to say about living. He wondered if God was like the man at the bottom of the river, or if God wore a grey uniform with a number printed under the words Angola State Prison, or if God carried a rifle and an attitude and rattled on the bars in the middle of the night. Sometimes he'd think about this while he was spading out sand, or turning up earth, or ringing his spade against a stone. It seemed to him that God was just a name like Emmaline and Raynelle—a name that made music inside his head.

The years began to wear out like the soles of his work boots. Most of the men he buried now were younger than him. Sometimes it made him tired and he wondered if he ought to dig out his own grave and just lie down in it, but he didn't do it. *Emmaline, Emmaline, Emmaline.* The spade and the roses and the names singing in his head.

One night at the near hind end of his years, the bootjacks came rattling at the bars. "Hey Spade," they called out, "Governor says you're a free man." He lay there listening, his eyes wide open, and him not saying a word. "Hey Spademan, you listening to us? Gov says you're walking outta here come Sunday." They rattled the bars some more, but he didn't move. He just tried out the words inside his head. They rattled the bars again, then moved off mumbling something angry.

Every night after that, every night right up to that Sunday, he dreamt about the river man, dreamt that he and the river man were scuffling, wrestling with each other deep down under the waters, struggling. He'd wake up sweaty, his lungs aching, hungry for breath.

Come Sunday, they took away his grey uniform, took away his boots with the worn down soles and gave him new clothes and new shoes. At midnight, the bootjacks came for him, two of them, like they do for the 'lectric chair men. They opened the door, but he didn't budge. "Come on," they said. But he didn't come on, he wasn't going to come on unless they gave him his spade. They said they couldn't do that, that the spade belonged to the Angola State Prison. But he didn't move, and finally one of them took the radio off his belt and spoke into it.

They gave him the spade—for forty years of faithful service. Then they walked him to the gate and pushed him out into the blackness, into the dark swirling torrents, into the flood.

When the sun emerged from the darkness and the waters grew quiet, he was standing on the front porch of a brown-faced woman, standing there holding some fool spade. The brown-faced woman, threw open the door. "Moreese," she sang.

The river man stepped into the light.

# Instructions to a Painter

*Donald Hall*

John Singer Sargent defined portraiture
as that genre of painting in which
there's always something a little wrong
about the mouth.
                              Pay small attention
to the slouching back, or to shoulders
that appear incapable of shouldering,
or to the middle's burgeoning convexity.
But give us the face full front, features
mobile enough for a moment's brush
of attention. Paint to give us the mouth,
possibly twisted a little, lips pursed,
full at the center, with thin twin downset
extensions, often quick or furtive.
Give us the large irregular nose, and jowls
that sag and flush. Give us a modest chin
that modestly conceals itself in puffs
of neck and jaw, projecting a skin-mole
that offers itself as the chin's chin.
Finally give us the eyes. By all means
give us the eyes in their black birdsnests
of skin, last year's eyries visible in April
after snow as spills of darkness and density
at the joints of branches, ruinous hovels
of worry and abuse, their former tenants
migrated south; or if they should return
in a wet spring, give us birds that lurk
and twitch in fibrous huts.
                              But a hand
must rise and hover to conceal the mouth,
which will require scraping and painting
again—or someone might find it out.

# The Icehouse

*Patrick Riley*

*Plantation in Virginia based on "The Ferry Hill Plantation Journal: January 4, 1838 - January 15, 1839" ©1961 University of North Carolina Press*

Daddy never brought on an overseer. He said he didn't need one, besides that would cost too much. Most of the slaves and the hired on help worked without any supervision other than Will, Ben or one of the other slave foremen, and that suited Daddy fine. And it wasn't a big plantation, but we had sheep for wool, bees for honey, cattle for milk, butter and meat, apples for cider and vinegar. Pretty much the same as everyone. Daddy rarely hit the slaves. He was really a kind man, mostly, much kinder than the other owners. He let the slaves walk alone into Sheperdstown to pick something up or buy some new clothes and he always trusted them with the money. I remember one time he even sent Ben into town with the wagon and a harrow that needed some fixing. Daddy figured it was less expensive to treat them right rather than bring on an overseer.

Oh sure, the slaves would get a little slacking every now and again or run away, but with a good description of what they were wearing, someone always returned them for the reward. Still, Daddy was disappointed when they ran away. Mostly things went along pretty well for a while, but that was when I was nothing but a little girl who loved ice.

Sometimes, during hot summer days, when we got all sweated up, Mother would give us children a few chips of ice to put under our tongues. We'd sit down in the shade of a poplar tree and watch the slow breezes comb the wheat grass first in one direction and then another. Those ice shavings, cold, slick bits of relief, would glide around our mouths until they disappeared into a cool trickle, soothing the back of our throats. I fell in love with ice in August.

Daddy never did any manual labor on the plantation. He was always studying the books or trying to figure out what to plant next or some other thing. That is, except for when it came to the icehouse. He, like me, loved ice in August and we always made it an outing to fill the icehouse during the frosty Virginia winters.

The icehouse was a deep pit dug into a tree-shaded hillside. Daddy had the slaves smooth-line it with bricks and dig it extra deep so that the ice would last at least through the summer. It was over 20 feet to the bottom, and I remember one year we even had ice and frozen custard on my birthday in October. A three-foot drainage hole at the bottom of the shaft let the melting water run out and down the side of the hill.

One February, when I was almost eleven-and-a-half, Jupe—one of our best slaves—hitched up the horses and brought the wagon around to the house. Daddy wore a heavy woolen coat over his suit with high upright collars that covered his jaw. I had a woolen dress with an extra cotton shift underneath. Daddy pulled my poke bonnet tight around my face, buttoned my wool coat, and together we climbed up into the wagon, next to Jupe, for the long ride through the forest and over to the ice pond. The other slaves would meet us there.

On the ride, the only sounds were the wind whistling through the poplars, the milling of snow under wagon wheels, and the strained pulls of leather harnesses. Daddy didn't say anything. His mind was occupied. For months all he talked about with the other owners who came by was what they called the crippling tariff of '28. President John Quincy Adams was the first from the northern states in two-and-a-half decades. They said he was out to punish the southern, growing states by increasing the taxes on imported machinery. Daddy was mad. He was mad, and he was silent.

When we arrived, Will, Ben, Ned and some of the other slaves were already cutting big slabs of ice from the shallow pond. They used axes and long wooden-poled ice hooks to separate the big square-cut sheets. Jupe backed up the wagon so the other slaves could fill it, and with straining backs and groans echoing, they did. Soon we were headed back through the forest toward the icehouse.

Before we arrived, little Jess, a slave about my age, had already been in the pit and cleaned out all the old, rotten sawdust and straw from the previous year. Using the drainage hole to climb through, little Jess had ready-access to the bottom of the icehouse. He lined it with fresh sawdust and was scampering back out the hole just as we pulled up.

Daddy got out of the wagon so that he could help position it. Jupe yelled at little Jess, telling him to get back to the barracks and sit by the fire because his clothes were wet and muddy from climbing through the drainage hole. Jupe then started to back the wagon over the steep side of the hill. It was harder to back-up the wagon this way, but it left the hind-end of it at a good incline over the edge of the pit. They would then open the wagon hatch, and it would be a small matter, using an ice hook, to slide the ice-slabs out and down into the hole.

I stood on the side of the hill, watching. For some reason, Daddy found himself pinned between the back-end of the wagon and the rim of the icehouse. Jupe couldn't see him and so kept coming on. Rather then cry-out, Daddy began a strange teetering motion on the edge. As he struggled to keep from falling backward into the pit, he clutched at the approaching wagon. Then he fell, yanking open the back hatch.

I screamed as Daddy fell into darkness. Jupe stopped. A dreadful thud rang-up and I froze. After several moments, Daddy called-out, saying he was all right, except for some pain or worse in his ankle. He told Jupe to get a rope or find some way to pull him out of the pit. He said it was cold and dark and only a little bit of light came down from the top. He sounded a little afraid. The smooth, damp surface of the brick-lined hole made it impossible for him to scale up the walls. So he yelled that Jupe would have to pull him back up.

I shouted that he could easily just crawl out the drainage hole just like little Jess did. He would be covered in mud and sawdust but he'd be out. I don't know if he didn't hear me, didn't want to copy little Jess, or was just too mad to think about it. Sometimes Daddy was like that. If he thought there was only one right answer, you couldn't talk to him otherwise. He just kept screaming at Jupe to go get a ladder or a rope or something.

Jupe was still in control of the wagon and had one foot on the brake while the back end hung over the hole. He looked like he didn't know what to do. He dared not leave the wagon on the hillside. Yet he couldn't ignore Daddy's screaming commands. Daddy only got more frustrated, hollered louder, and Jupe looked more helpless. I kept going on about the drainage hole.

Jupe set the wagon brake, then climbed down and ran toward one of the barns to look for a rope. He didn't get more than a couple of steps before the brake let loose with a loud clatter of wood and metal. The horses, feeling the wagon start to run down the hill, bolted ahead. They yanked at it with such effort that the ice began sliding off the back. I screamed.

As the great tablets of ice tottered and fell down into the pit, I heard Daddy yell Jupe's name. Only once. Only once but the echo of it seemed to last forever. When half a wagonload of ice had slid down into the icehouse, I sat down on the hard ground near the pit and cried. I just cried. Didn't know what else to do. Jupe circled around, gaping into the pit and looking in wide-eyed disbelief at what had happened. He worked a finger into his ear, like he was trying to pull the echo of Daddy's shouting from his mind. After another few minutes of my sobbing, Jupe took off, running away through the trees. I saw him run.

Jupe probably couldn't see any other way out, so he ran. Ran until he couldn't run anymore.

They found him a couple days later, huddled in a barn in

Sharpsburg. Mother said she didn't want to see Jupe again, so they shot him right there in the barn. No investigation. No nothing. I had tried to talk to Mother; I told her it wasn't Jupe's fault. Daddy was thinking about other things and got pinned behind the wagon. But she wouldn't listen.

They figured Ned must have ferried Jupe across the Potomac or else Jupe couldn't have gotten into Maryland. Mother had Ned shot for conspiring to help another slave escape. I cried. Didn't know what else to do.

Once Ned, Jupe and Daddy were gone, the slaves started running away all the time. Mother didn't know what to do so she hired an overseer, a cruel man who beat them continuously, and, well, let me just say that those were the years when I grew up. Those were the years when I started to think about things.

At some point, I realized that maybe none of us were ever really happy there. Maybe we were all in some play where everyone's lines are set and no matter how much we want to change, we can't because we can only see a small bit of light. No matter how many times people tell us that there is another, better way, we don't or can't hear them because we're scared. We believe that there is only one answer, one way out—slick walls mask the truth—and so we stare ahead, push ahead.

I started to think, maybe the whole War Between the States was like that, and after my oldest boy was killed near Antietam Creek—not far from where Jupe died—I was sure. We were all standing at the bottom of that icehouse.

# Cop School

*Helen L. Campbell*

It wasn't the first lie Jed Barton had ever told, or the biggest, but it certainly must have been one of the *dumbest*. I stared at him, watching his stringy gray beard bob up and down as he told me, for the second time, his version of the crime.

"See, Sheriff Wilbur, ma'am, they was two of 'em. They come runnin' out of the field and they clumb up that there rail fence, then hightailed it on down the road."

"On foot?" I asked, fighting back a grin. Being Kudzu County's first female sheriff was usually an uphill battle, but it had its lighter moments.

"Well, yuh. Then this car pulled outta' the trees down there." He pointed a bony, nicotine-stained finger toward a grove of scrubby oaks.

I reached into my back pocket and pulled out the notepad and pen combo Kudzu County's D.A.—my brother, Harold—gave me when I graduated from the Law Enforcement Academy last month. I flipped it open.

"Can you describe the vehicle?"

"Let's see. It was a beat-up Chevy. Had a bashed-in fender."

On the first clean page of my tablet, I sketched in the opening strokes of a hangman game.

"Color?"

He hesitated, his eyes on my notepad. Luckily, from where he stood, he couldn't see what I was writing.

"Uh, blue."

I drew a perfectly round head, marveling at the same

40

time how glibly old Jed could conjure up such intricate details—about something that never happened. I polished off my diagram with a noose, then slipped the book back into my pocket. Out of the corner of my eye, I could see Jed track every move I made. It was all I could do to keep from laughing.

Then, with the touch of reverence Kudzu County citizens usually reserve for encyclopedia salesmen and faith healers, he asked, "Did you larn that in cop school–takin' notes an' stuff like that?"

"Yup," I replied, wishing I'd thought to add a magnifying glass to my crime kit.

I crossed the dusty road, keeping my attention on the ground, as if searching for imaginary clues. Jed followed, his head down, his matted, untidy beard resting against his chest.

"Hmm. Plenty of footprints."

He flinched. "Footprints? Oh, yuh, they's a lot of 'em." He glanced at his scuffed, run-down boots, then nervously hopped onto the grassy berm.

When I reached the fence that separated Slim Wilkens' watermelon field from Slick Creek Road, I stopped and looked over it. Slim had called the office about a week ago and asked me to keep an eye on his crop of melons. Someone had been pilfering them. He called again this morning and said if I didn't do something right away he was going to load up his shotgun and take care of it himself. So I headed on over. And found Jed at the scene. The minute I had seen him, I figured out what was going on. But I couldn't help wanting to have a little fun with him first.

I crawled between the rails of the fence and surveyed the damage. Footprints, the same as those in the dust, led from vine to vine. Chunks of what had once been two fat melons lay on the ground. Most of the sweet centers were eaten away, but on one of them there were deep indentations where fingers had sunk into the juicy red flesh.

I pointed. "Ought to be able to get some good fingerprints off those."

Jed, looking over my shoulder, jammed his hands into his pants pockets. I anticipated his next question.

"Yes, I learned that in cop school, too," I said.

It was a mighty worried man that trailed me back to my car.

"When did you say this happened?" I asked, breaking the edgy silence.

"Not mor'n an hour ago. I was just saunterin' down the road here, mindin' my own business . . . " He stopped. "You think you'll catch those guys?"

I nodded my head. "Certainly. No doubt about that. I've got all the evidence I need."

He glanced nervously at the .38 Smith & Wesson holstered on my belt.

"What's gonna happen to 'em?"

Casually, I rested my palm on the butt of the gun. To my knowledge, watermelon rustling had never been a capital crime, but I wasn't quite finished with this world-champion prevaricator.

"Well . . . " I started, watching him rock back and forth on his heels and scratch at the messy bird's nest on his chin. It was surprising how much you could learn about a man from the condition of his beard.

Deciding I'd let him stew long enough, I answered, "Not a whole lot. Probably if they apologize to Mr. Wilkens—maybe offer to help around the farm for a couple of days—*and* promise to leave his melons alone, I won't even have to arrest them.

"Otherwise," I added, shaking my head sadly, "I'm afraid I'll have to put the cuffs on them and haul them off to the jail."

Jed digested *that* little morsel for a minute or two. Then he said, "Ms. Sheriff, ma'am, I wanna' make a confession."

Although his statement didn't surprise me, his explanation did. "I been helping myself to these here melons for nigh on ten years and old Sheriff Briggs never did figger out who was doin' it. 'Course," he said, respectfully, "he ain't never been to cop school."

42

I loaded the light-fingered melon thief into my car and delivered him to Slim Wilkens' place. I waited until he'd delivered his apology, then left him there to work out the details of his penance. At last, on the way back to town, I gave in to the laughter I'd kept bottled up all morning. As Jed had rightly said, I'd benefited a great deal from my law enforcement training. But, it hadn't taken a cop school education to spot the half-dozen watermelon seeds tangled in the thatch of Jed Barton's beard.

# The Spray and the Slamming Sea

*Paul Lindholdt*

For five days a choppy bay has hidden the body of my
son. The newspapers say he is presumed drowned. My reverence for water deepens every hour. Now the blood is sound-
ing in my ears like waves on the shore—salt for salt, thud for
thud.

Braden was kayaking with his best friend in Puget Sound
at Larrabee Beach, a spot unique for its sandstone cliffs whose
wave-etched scarps remind my eye of veins and ribs. It was
March 11, 2001, still early in the year for paddling, the weather
unsteady. The guys promised their moms they'd stay close
to shore, off Chuckanut Drive near Bellingham, to make up
for the life vest neither wore. That was the last anyone saw
of them. The next day their boats washed up across the bay.

Six feet and four inches tall, buzz-cut and bullet-headed,
he plays basketball with skill and flair. *Played!* Before he van-
ished, he was going to college. A paper lay on his desk, ready
to hand in. An artist of the pen, he taught himself to sketch.
At the age of three he sketched me—the whiskered neck
unshamed by blade, the wire-rim glasses askew, the bed-head
hair. Savagely we cared for each other, father and son. Now
every glimpse of seawater rocks me, menaces me, unlike any
other vision ever did.

When I was a child in Seattle my father saved me from
death by water. Fishing on a river beside him, I remember
slipping and plunging into the drink. Minnows regarded me,

a clumsy creature flung into their nimble midst. Those seconds spent estranged in water did not terrorize me, though. The swim was liberating, almost sensual, though I was scarcely four. Before the water could carry me away, sweep me out to sea, my daddy's strong arm straightened, collared and hauled me back to wholesome light and air.

Two decades later I asked him for details about that close call, for the name of the river. Surprised, he told me it never happened, I did not slip, the ordeal took place only in my mind. How could that be? My memory of my swim was much too vivid to discredit.

Maybe I died in a previous life—if I choose to open the door to reincarnation. Or maybe it was all a dream, a precaution, harbinger of some sudden plunge to come.

Nearly one hundred searchers, all volunteers, tramp the beaches, knock on doors, and ply the waters of Puget Sound in the days after Jim and Braden disappear. Helicopter pilots scan the San Juan archipelago, giving their time freely, taking more than 20 flights. *Disappeared. Presumed drowned. Missing.* Lacking any certainty or evidence, his mother and I can plan no funeral, no burial. We wait in mystery and limbo, no closure in view.

Braden's favorite watch cap is found upon a beach. Vicki, my ex-wife, clings to me, drops rapid tears, and wrings the damp cap dry. Her sorrow has no bottom. I have come across the Cascades from Spokane, the first I have seen her in two years. Her face is swollen, barely recognizable, a product of prescription drugs and grief. She stoops.

Overwhelmed with longing and nostalgia, she won't switch off his computer. She grates at anyone who tries his bedroom door. She guards his urine crystallizing on the bathroom floor. Baseboard heat makes her home close, so I go for a walk above Larrabee.

Hikers hike at different rates. Some hikers like to hustle from start to stop, vying for new elapsed times, covering ground. I go slowly, snuffing the air, regarding birdcalls, even out the window of my moving car. I poke along, scrutinizing insects, inviting the lay of the land to invest itself in me. I can stare at a tuft of lupines a long time, charged by the way each leaf cup cradles rain, idly guessing when the tiptop of the flower head might grow ponderous enough to nod.

A trail shaded by maples and firs terraces a hill above Larrabee. Through the Earth's thin crust, tough mushrooms shove, splintering fallen tree trunks, crumbling concrete where need be. In my fragile state, fungi wield tremendous power. I pluck one, a prince mushroom, *Agaricus augustus*, its broad cap curving to upturned gills. It smells like trees. How fully mushrooms, those torpid flesh-flowers, flourish on death and decay.

The Kiowa writer N. Scott Momaday encourages "reciprocal appropriation" of the land, whereby a being respectfully surrenders to the landscape and takes it into his experience. Maybe that's what Braden did—too enthusiastically. If the *–scape* of "landscape" is scope, and scope suggests knowledge, then Braden knows the watery landscape at Larrabee Beach well. Knows it organically, not consciously. Knows it like a fallen leaf knows rain.

During Braden's time in the womb, Mount St. Helens blew. We were camping near the town of Oroville, far north of the exploded mountain, but we heard the blast as though it were a mining charge a mile away. A radio report confirmed what happened. Vicki insisted that we flee home, first south and then west, across Stevens Pass to get to Puget Sound. The sheltering Cascades rose in advance of the mile-high curtain of ash.

In those days we camped and hiked a lot. In bear country, she had been afraid. And so I packed a handgun with us on some jaunts. One night in eastern Montana, in tornado season and terrain, a thunderstorm passed very close. The lightning's flash and thunder's crack were simultaneous events. The tent poles shone like ribs, the nylon sheath like a thin red skin. That pistol beneath the pack, that tool I toted for safety's sake, afforded her no comfort in the storm. She yodeled fear in dreams or could not sleep.

Vicki and I grieve at different rates. Hers is swift and physical, groaning, low, a blow as though from a kayak paddle jabbed to the solar plexus. My own pace on the path towards calm is a fumbling and tunneled vision, numb and vulnerable in open space.

Ten days have passed. Water haunts my rest each night. Allured by it, repulsed too, I hear its call—Triton, Shiva, an Old Testament lord all anger and caprice. From my waking dream I watch its fluid moods. To escape it I cower, but the water is booming, flashing, a tsunami poised to slam above my puny spit of sand. A dream-steed rides me, a nag whose hoofs keep relaxation distant, who rejoices that rivers do not sleep, waves never relent, the moon pulls irrepressibly, rain falls and evaporates, with or without me.

Many times I have cheated water's partner, death. The closest escape came in 1979, the year before Braden was born, while salmon fishing off the Strait of Juan de Fuca. It was May. The kings were running. Black mouths, silver sides, full of hunger and fight. They schooled beyond the mouth of Puget Sound, where the warlike Pacific throws its weight around. We nosed toward naked ocean aboard an eighteen-foot inboard.

The boat's owner, Fred, had some knowledge of ocean waves. To earn his aqua-lungs, Fred had worked as a skipper for dudes out of Westport, before he sold his soul to Boeing. But Fred liked to get too stoned for most comfort zones. With frantic care he guided his boat one-handed, smoking a reefer with the other, often tilting a beer.

The waves loomed large once we departed the harbor at Neah Bay, the same harbor famed today as a put-in point for whalers in the Makah tribe. We headed out that day in May, plunging along the whale-road, the sky clear, Vancouver Island at our backs, no wind to worry us, balancing on swells already human-high. Tatoosh Island passed to starboard and we entered open sea—*la mere*, wine-dark, prehistoric mother of us all.

Fred set aside his drink and smoke to thread a cut-plug

herring on his line. One hook passed through the hollow gut of the bait-fish, emerging near its anal vent, the other bristling where the head should be. A five-ounce lead weight plummeted the line and the bait through the chop, which was already towering taller than our staggered craft.

"Put your lines in!" Fred hissed, his words an audible function of the spray and slamming sea. The skipper knew fish were there. He had seen a rip tide. The phantoms of king salmon agitated him. Presently his pole bent, and he handed the steering wheel to me. "Keep it facing the waves," he commanded, legs spread, horsing in the slug Chinook.

Cresting and lunging with random shifts in pitch, the boat mounted the wall of each successive swell, then plunged back to wallow in the trough before the next wave came. Seasick weather, our faces paled. A kind of claustrophobia ensues in heavy seas. Walls of water rise on every side, the skies shut down, and the light grows emerald and probes. One source of motion sickness in the human body is the ear, its salty water there.

The rollers came sloping, now eighteen and twenty feet in height. Backlit walls of green foam filtered light from the hidden sky, silhouetting fish like bugs in amber. Our stomachs clenched. Schools of herring swam above us, bent on spawning in the calm of Puget Sound. As if jeering, silhouettes of king salmon overtopped the deck, wave-tossed, heedless of the threat of getting caught broadside. Half the time our lines were slanting up above us. Weary and scared, my mates and I feared another boat might hit us, a wind might rise and slash the wave crests, and whitecaps might fling water to the deck. We threatened to mutiny. Capitulating with a sorry snarl, Fred wheeled the boat around.

Thoughts of Braden's final moments taunt me. My stomach cracks and growls like far-off thunder, gnawing at itself, fraying the sleeves of sleep. I have been trying to read philosophy, just turned off the lamp, and a tide of advice from the *Enchiridion* rises.

Epictetus, the Roman slave who wrote that book of consolation, spoke in loaded language of the transience of life. "On a voyage," he noted, "when the ship is at anchor, if you disembark to get water, you may amuse yourself by picking up a stone or a shell on the beach. But your thoughts ought to be on the ship every minute, to be always attentive, for fear the captain should call, and then you must leave all your things behind."

Unlike the Greek and Roman Stoics, I rely on spoken words to get me through. If the Ancient Mariner told his story to absolve himself, I lean on speech to air my grief. My mouth a vent, a compression release, eases the tension in my head. The mariner in the poem by Coleridge kills an albatross and pays hard penance by wearing its corpse around his neck, wandering the high seas, and telling his pain to anyone who'll heed him.

"The Ancient Mariner" is a sonorous swatch of sorrow about the sea. So is much of America's literature—from Poe's Pym, to Melville's Ishmael, to Whitman's "cradle, endlessly rocking." The heedless sea, creator and destroyer, redeemer and swift doom.

Two weeks after Braden's cap turns up on the sand, I am buckling on a life jacket. Alex, Derrick, and Neil tote their canoes and kayaks to the bank of tiny, swift Rock Creek. My hands are trembling at the jacket clasps. These young men, students and friends, have scanned the maps and hiked the cliffs above the Eastern Washington stream. Alex and Derrick are thrilled to be here. For seven hours we will dodge rocks, portage past falls and logs, and clamber slopes to pictographs scrawled on basalt walls.

No one knows for sure where we're going, only where we parked the shuttle car. No one in our party has paddled this stream before. At the shuttle drop-off spot a farmer, a red-faced Marlboro smoker with swollen ankles and scared hair, calls us crazy for tackling this stretch of water, this stony plunge through canyons fed by Rock Lake.

I push the bow of my boat out. Flycatchers and magpies flit and gather sticks for nests. It is still the month of March.

Storm clouds threaten rain, although Rock Creek in this drought year is barely navigable—narrow, twisting, boulder-strewn. Fences cross it; fallen trees, called strainers or sweepers, can stop and swamp unwatchful boaters with the current's force. Herds of mule deer file the hillsides, ears twitching, gazing over shoulders as they go. Someplace in some sudden canyon, none of us is sure exactly where, a fifty-foot waterfall will obstruct our way.

My kayak knifes its way downstream. Nearly at the water level, I sit so low as to be part of the flow, an integer in nature's equation. I stroke right, gouge left, and lean the molded plastic craft before each turn. We're in class-one whitewater, non-technical, a piece of cake. Waves spray over the gunwale, wetting faces and arms and legs. Besides our life jackets, known among river rats as PFDs for personal flotation devices, we are wearing no special helmets, dry suits or other gear. Hanging branches bruise us. Our muscles strain. Exhilaration and anxiety mix freely, compounding the fatigue and chill.

On one sudden right-hand hairpin, in a pool scooped at the base of steepling basalt columns, Alex and Neil capsize. Almost instantly they bob to the surface, holding paddles in one hand and the canoe in the other. They ride out the turn, before pulling up on a grassy bank to pour the stream back out. Their clothing will be dampish for the day.

Neil, like me, has water issues to confront. He, too, trembles. Seven years before this trip, he watched both his younger brother and best friend go down in Lake Roosevelt, the reservoir formed of the Columbia River below Grand Coulee Dam.

Near the burg of Keller the boys were hand-paddling inner tubes of tractor tires, three of them, to reach an island the dam had exposed. Mid-channel a wicked wind arose. The tires were stripped from their grip, sent rolling end over end, and they were left with nothing to trust but muscle power. Neil, a weight lifter and football player then, urged the others to work the water hard, he called to them to keep the faith, but no amount of urging could give them strength and warmth to stroke to shore. They cried out several times and then surrendered, "almost peaceful," Neil said, to hypothermia and fatigue.

My tortured imagination tells me that this is probably how Braden drowned. Wisely Neil did not try to rescue his drowning kin. The drowning swimmer often drowns the one who would save him. Panic sets in. It could have been that Jim, Braden's partner, who had broken his legs in a motorcycle crash two years before, was flailing and Braden tried to help him. Maybe both of them were dashed unconscious on the cliffs.

A month has passed. It's April 12. To get some rest, I turn to memories of him.

My son was intrepid enough to travel the West with me in a series of low-budget adventures. In an Oregon desert I cooked raw oysters over a juniper fire. Those oysters quivered on Braden's plate. They were snotty and chewy, charred and underdone, but he ate them and said I was a good cook.

Another time, beside a tent high in Nevada, at Great Basin National Park where millennia-old bristlecone pines grow, a herd of beef cows came thundering into our camp and almost flattened him. He was scared. He wet his pants. At least that's what an old photo shows. But he slept there with me in that tent, and as I remember he slept well.

He also rested on a thin canvas cot, spindly with aluminum legs, beside me for a week in Deary, Idaho, while we cared for a farm and 80 acres. Each night before we got in bed, we watched the mountains turn purple and heard the great-horned owls hoot. Then we checked each other's scalp for ticks that helped themselves to suppers of our blood.

There was another time, another long drive, all the way to Disneyland, sleeping at campgrounds and eating fast food. The first night in that plastic province we had some fish at a restaurant and took turns heaving at the motel toilet till after midnight. The next day he was cheerful enough to mug for my camera beside a wax-museum figure of Mr. T.

And we had dangerous times together—like driving the

North Cascades Highway and hitting a mule deer that nearly crashed through the car windshield, like colliding with a runaway pickup wheel that disabled our Honda wagon on Interstate 5. After dark on foot we crossed those busy freeway lanes, southbound and northbound alike, holding hands and running hard and dodging cars, to reach a lighted rest stop on the other side.

Sleep returns after two months; it ravels back my tattered sleeves. In Bellingham we hold a memorial service. At that service Braden's friends and family speak. I stand up and speak, unsure at first if I can pull it off. My four-year-old son, Reed, takes the hand of his sobbing aunt and looks her in the eye. He and Braden had swum together.

Now it is July. Vicki says she hopes he won't be found—skeletal, decayed—rather that he be left alone. I agree, if only for her sake. Let him stay in Puget Sound, cushioned by seaweed, rocked by storms and tides. Finding him would be an irruption of the organic cycle. Instead we parents will erect a bench above the beach. That bench will warn off the ill-equipped, the innocent, the invincible. And it will honor our sons.

# Litany

*Diane Averill*

(for Kelsey)

Bless the seal that surfaces
out of the tissues of the sea
and bless the sea that contains
both salt and weed.
Bless the arched spine of
the not-yet-born baby as it rises
from the surface of my
daughter's belly and bless
the belly itself, growing
more slowly than a swell in the ocean.
Bless the snowy plover turning
in the foam at the edge of the waves.
like laughter released at the borders
of the psyche, and bless the psyche
which accepts that laughter.

Take the offerings of the breakers
and of the uterus.
Take the milk which echoes
clouds and blue rain.
Take the smallest bones of the sea
and assemble them in your own order.
Then take that order and arrange it
to cry for the night.
Take night and give it back to day.
And bless the day which steps forward
to make itself known.

# The Flooded Forest

*Nnedi Okorafor*

Few who live in the forest are old enough to have witnessed the great floods. Those who are were too young to remember it specifically. But the great floods have survived in the stories passed from generation to generation.

There's one story that's especially memorable.

When the floodwaters last invaded the land, it was a time of loss; for everything had to be left behind. It was best to simply accept it, as was always the case when it comes to nature. Few would return until the waters were completely gone. Those that did return only did so out of great necessity because strange things were known to accompany the rising waters.

The forest flooded quickly under the deluge of rains, and the world was turned upside down. Where birds once perched, fish competed for food. Crabs and shrimps hid underneath leaves where insects and spiders once made their homes. Catfish nibbled at the waterlogged tree trunks and hippos and river cows—the people of the water—feasted on leaves they'd never tasted.

Umuzau arrived with the other sea creatures. She was equally as curious.

This is Umuzau's story. And one other whom this story will eventually reach. Enjoy the waters for a moment. The story will take care of itself.

Umuzau was only ninety years old, and this was her first

chance to finally see the forest and the village. She'd watched the village from the rising rivers as the people had loaded as much as they could carry onto boats. Umuzau was sure they must have left many things behind. Their boats weren't very big.

She wasn't interested in people who couldn't swim, who chopped down trees and built boats that roared and tore up the backs of the river cows. But she was interested in their things.

Umuzau lived a serene life in the river, eating fish, sleeping and visiting with friends, none of whom were like herself. It had been this way most of her life. She only remembered her parents from when she was very young. They taught her how to speak above and below the water. Then one day they were fished out of the sea. She tumbled from her mother's arms and she never saw her parents again. A river cow had found and raised her.

Every few months, she'd grow restless and follow the river a hundred miles to the sea where she swam deep, inhaling the salt water. But she always returned to the same mile of river where she had been born.

Only when there was a good reason did she come up for air. Taking air into her gills was like swallowing frozen nettles. She'd once bore the cold sting in her throat for several minutes so that she could watch a shiny metallic object floating on the surface, reflecting the sun.

She had coiled it up and wrapped it around her wrist, enjoying the contrast of the shiny silver object against her black skin. She closed her eyes, tilted her head back and enjoyed the warmth of the odd sun. Her bleached red eels of hair slapped at her back. She shivered in the warmth and dove back into the water before her skin dried out. The tinfoil bracelet had lasted for a few weeks before it fell off one day.

Now she circled loops around the tree branches. As she swam though sunbeams, the reflections of her tail's shiny scales dotted the trees and creatures around her. She often wondered if her love for sparkling things came from her love of herself.

She swam with speed, excited to get to the village. The houses were made of cement and adobe and green in the wavering filtered sunlight. They looked as if they had always been under water. There were vehicles parked in front of a few of them. She'd seen vehicles as they drove down the roads close to the river. They were clumsy hulking things that moved like insecure hippos. She tapped at one's side mirrors and pulled at things until she figured out how to open it. A large bubble flew out of it like a freed ghost. A crocodile quickly swam into the car when she left.

She swam to a house, looked inside, opened a window and swam in. In a drawer, she found shiny pieces of metal and she clicked them together, enjoying the hard sturdy sound. It was the only thing humans were good at, making and collecting hard things.

She went from house to house, doing much of the same. She found pots, pans, knives, CDs, books, light bulbs, televisions.

She found the real prize in the brown house. She was tearing out the pages of a soggy book when it caught her eye. The prize was in a corner. At first she thought it was one of those wonderful metallic colored fish that she loved to watch swim about. But those fish never stopped moving.

She swam down to see. The silver pendant necklace was the color of the sky and the shape of a fish's eye. She held it up in the light and watched it twinkle. Lovely, she thought. She put it around her neck, laughed a series of delighted bubbles and was off.

She was almost through the window when she saw him. He was only a few feet away. He must have seen her first. His eyes were wide, and as she looked at him, he lost his last gulp of air. He turned and made for the surface.

His name was Issa and at the age of nineteen, the son of a long line of fisherman, he was an expert swimmer. He was also a very rational boy. Thus, his father didn't fight too hard to keep him from doing what he was doing. His father knew that Issa wasn't likely to do anything that would get him killed. The rational reaction to fish people was to retreat, very very quickly.

Umuzau watched him frantically swim straight up. He swam swiftly for a creature without fins. She squinted trying to get a good look at his legs. He was swimming to his boat, which floated near the top of a tall palm tree. He was the first human being she'd ever been close to. So strange looking. She decided to follow.

His body gave off a most panicked scent. He was terrified of her and this made her more curious. Though he swam fast for a human, Umuzau had no trouble catching up. She was a foot away from his kicking feet when he scrambled out of the water and threw himself into his small boat.

He was puffing heavily, frantically searching for his paddle as he kept his body at the boat's center, when she broke the water's surface. Paddle in hand, Issa screamed and was about to plunge the paddle into the water and push hard when he froze.

He was held by her lidless brown black eyes. Then his eyes migrated to the rest of her. Her forehead was crinkled with curiosity. Her nose was ribbed with white cartilage that contrasted greatly with her black skin. She was like some sort of snake, her skin overwhelmingly smooth, ribs of cartilage running from her neck, between her small breasts to the start of her fin that sparkled pastel blue, yellow, pink and green with scales.

All these observations normally would have made him frantically attempt to paddle away as quickly as his muscular arms could propel him. But it was the necklace she wore around her neck that caused him not to attempt an escape. He stared at it for a long while, then he sighed. His shoulders slumped. He didn't know what to do.

Umuzau cocked her head to the side as she stared at his face. Her skin always had a thin oily substance coating it for speed and protection. Though he was wet, his skin still seemed dry. And his face was so blank, no ridges of cartilage. His skin was a dark brown, not black. She moved forward so that she could look at his legs in the boat, and he whimpered. She stopped and looked up at him. He stared back.

"What's the matter with you?" she asked.

The boy gasped and clapped his hands over his ears and almost fell out of his boat. Umuzau smiled when she understood. Her words hurt his ears. She'd tried to speak to a hippo this way once and it had roared, and then scrambled out of the water.

She took a breath and then addressed him in the above-water language she had not used since she was a child.

"What is wrong with you?" she asked. She spoke slowly, the language feeling unfamiliar.

He blinked but relaxed a bit.

"What is wrong with you?" she said again, this time more quickly.

"What are you?" he asked, his hand grasping his paddle tightly.

Umuzau paused and then said, "I am Umuzau. What are you?"

He frowned and then said, "I'm Issa."

"Issa," she said. "You act like you are fish and...I am crocodile."

"The necklace," he said. "Why are you wearing it? It's why I'm here."

Umuzau bobbed in the water trying to process his words. Her throat felt dry and her skin was beginning to sting.

"I will be back," she said. She dove into the water, shivering as her skin became wet again. Then she resurfaced. He looked at her, this time with less terror and more curiosity.

"I found this," she said, touching the necklace. "Down below. It my first time in village. It is new and interesting."

"It's mine," Issa said. "It belonged to my mum. It must have fallen on the floor when we were fleeing the rains."

"Can you not get another one for her?"

"My mum is gone," he said.

"Where?" she asked.

"She..." he shook his head and looked into her eyes and said, "She's dead."

Umuzau frowned, she thought of her mother, whom she had only known for the first decade of her life. Who was also probably dead. She had nothing of her mother's or her father's.

"It is beautiful," she said taking it off. She swam up to give it to him. Then she moved backwards and smiled. "Come to the water and I will give to you."

Issa looked down at the water and then at Umuzau. She was so strange. He was brown but she was black. Even in her face she looked part fish. But now that he'd had a little time to look at her, he found a peacefulness about her; his instinct told him that she would not murder him. He looked at the necklace and then took a chance. Even if she were evil, he wouldn't be able to get away in his small boat. It was over two miles to land. Slowly, he climbed into the water.

Umuzau laughed and immediately went underwater to see how his legs paddled to keep him afloat. He swam well but he was made for land. She pinched one of his toes and, above, she heard him yelp. He shouldn't be here, she thought. For the time being, this place was her territory.

"You should not be here," she said coming to the surface.

"My mum's necklace," he said, motioning to her neck.

She touched the necklace and looked down at it. Then she took it off and held it out to him.

He slowly took the necklace from her, his nose tingling at her water plant and salty smell. He reached forward with his other hand and Umuzau didn't move away. He touched her cheek and then looked at his fingers. They were slick with clear oil. He decided she smelled wonderful.

Umuzau reached forward and pinched his cheek hard.

"Ouch!"

"Your skin is dry," she said. He smelled as she thought humans would smell. Like smoke.

"Yours is oily," he said.

They bobbed in the water staring at each other.

Issa thought about all the fish people stories he'd heard. That they were evil demons with no religion or morals. That they would pull their victims under the water and watch them drown. That they had no real language. Only a language like the dolphins that, when heard above water, would cause ears to bleed.

Umuzau didn't remember where she got her beliefs about humans, but she was sure that they were awkward in the water. That they were simple minded and destructive. When large numbers of fish died or she heard trees fall, it was because of them. The males especially, would scream like children when they saw one of her kind and flee, returning equipped with weapons.

They both knew better now.

"Issa," Umuzau said.

"Yes?"

"The air grows uncomfortable for me," she said. "I must go."

Issa nodded.

"Will you come back to the river after the water retreats?" he asked.

"Yes," she said. She scooped some water into her palm and drank it to sooth her throat. "Will you return to this village?"

"Yes," he said.

Umuzau was about to dive back into the water when Issa said, "Can I come and see you...at the river?"

Umuzau smiled.

"You can find me where the river bends when the sun is out and the air is wet." She paused and then said, "I like shiny things."

Issa watched her dive back into the water, his mother's necklace in his hand. He blinked a few times, staring down at the crystal clear water, trying to see where she went. She was gone. Even more quickly than she appeared. His people were fisherman and the love for the water ran in his blood. Now the waters were even more mysterious.

He climbed into his boat looking back one more time over his flooded village and the flooded forest. It was a terrifying and amazing sight to see it all underwater.

"Umuzau," he whispered, like bubbles of magic from his lips.

He would realize that he had fallen in love in exactly seven days. Umuzau would realize it in two weeks.

They met again a month later. Umuzau showed him the mysteries of the water. Issa brought her shiny thing after shiny thing and anything with buttons, that ran on batteries, or had knobs and dials. And they talked into the night and created new myths together where human beings could breath under water and fish people could fly.

And when the forest flooded again, after Issa had grown into an old man and passed on and Umuzau had long since swam into the sea in search of new things, three fish people flocked to the forest with the other water creatures to see what they could see of the legendary Umuzau and Issa's land village, where so many famous stories originated, especially the story of Issa and Umuzau. To this day, the people of Issa's village still tell the story of Umuzau and Issa, the water and land deities of the old days.

Like the water, stories are. And like land is life. When a forest becomes flooded the result is like a juju man's strongest juju.

✦╾═◎◎═╼✦

# A Tale of Two Livers

*Ann Adams*

My mother wants me to give her part of my liver. She's an alcoholic dying of cirrhosis, and doctors can do that now. The liver regenerates itself. They can cut a chunk out of my liver and put it into my mother to replace her booze-ravaged liver.

The drawback is that I could die in the process. The knife could slip, or the doctors could miss sewing up one of the blood vessels they have to cut to get to my liver. Do you think my mother cares about that? Let me tell you her reasoning: She had me in the first place to keep her marriage together, but when I was five, my father left anyway, and she has never let me forget it. When she has been really drunk, she has accused me of driving my father away. When she has been slightly soberer, she has only said, in a regretful tone, that I just didn't measure up, I just wasn't good enough to keep him around.

This is the most recent opportunity she has given me to make it up to her. Over the years she has given me opportunity after opportunity, but though I always tried hard, I could never do it.

I'm a slow learner. I was 30 years old when I stopped trying. What I did was tell her to get permanently lost, and I moved 3,000 miles away from her, to the other coast. I should have kept going on over to Hawaii. Or to Australia, to the Outback where they don't have telephones.

When the phone rang, my digital clock said 3 a.m. "Honey, it's Mom," she said into my startled ear.

"Mom who?" I said, turning on the light. I hadn't heard

from her in 10 years. I thought it was my recurring nightmare.

"This is Ophelia Thomas Richardson," she snapped. "Your mother."

"I don't have a mother," I said and hung up.

Phil turned his light on and sat up. He took my shaking hand and held it steady.

The phone rang again. "Tell me this is a dream," I said.

"It's not a dream," he said.

What I love about Phil is that he doesn't give advice. He waits quietly for me to tell him what I've decided to do. And he never asks me to explain why I do or feel anything.

But he listens to everything I say.

The phone rang some more, and he waited for me to decide what to do about it. I picked it up. "Let me guess," I said. "You just wrecked your car, and you want me to come get you. I'll bet you have in front of you the flight schedule from SeaTac. I'll bet you've reserved a ticket for me, having wormed my credit card number out of an FBI agent you met in a bar."

"What? What are you talking about? Are you trying to be funny? Nobody likes a smart aleck. I ought to hang up on you."

"But I'll bet your maternal instinct, your generous spirit, is going to keep you from doing that. I'll bet your generous spirit, your maternal instinct, is goading you to give me another opportunity to redeem myself. What do you want now?"

The receiver tinkled. "You always make me laugh, in spite of myself. You're a charmer. A real con artist. Like your father."

I gurgled. "Have you heard from my father? Is this about my father?"

"No, it's not about your father. It's about your mother. Your soon-to-be-deceased mother. I'm dying."

That was a new one. She'd never pulled that one before.

"Unless," she said.

And then she told me about the liver opportunity.

I got the next flight to New York from SeaTac. Ophelia (I refuse to call her "Mother") was at New York University Medical Center. Phil wanted to go with me. He was just before being pushy. I suppose we all act out of character when the crunch comes. I acted out of character, too. Phil is my rock, my lifeline, my link to sanity. Since we were married 10 years ago, I'd never spent a night away from him. But this was something I had to Do By Myself.

"I want to tell her 'no' to her face," I said. "And I want her to know it comes from me, not you."

"A woman's gotta do what a woman's gotta do," Phil said. But he packed a bag before he drove me to the airport, just in case I changed my mind at the last minute.

Ophelia sat up in the hospital bed, shrunken and sallow against the white pillows. Her big brown eyes floated like marbles in egg custard. She looked up at me under chocolate-colored bangs which were gray at the roots. Her nose was big in her tiny oval face, and her wrinkles were out. She used to yell at my father that if he made more money, she could get her nose fixed and she wouldn't need to drink to feel socially acceptable.

"Socially acceptable" had to be the first English words I ever heard. Maybe I didn't know what they meant, but how could I ever forget their rhythm and their sound? If the doctors opened up my brain instead of my liver, I have no doubt that they would find the words "socially acceptable" carved there.

She looked so pitiful that I went over to kiss her. She wrinkled her nose. "Have you brushed your teeth?" she said. My eyes must have hardened (they felt like they did) because she grabbed me and pulled me down to kiss me on the lips. I was startled. Her lips were like dry rose petals, and her breath had no trace of bourbon.

She pushed me away as if the kiss had been a bad idea, and I knew I wasn't in the wrong room.

"You look like something the cat dragged in," she said.

"I haven't had much sleep," I said, pulling myself together.

"Well, go get some coffee," she said. "And put on some lipstick. You need to be alert to talk to the doctor. He's coming in at 1, and it's 12:30 now. You took your time getting here."

"I'm fine, thanks for asking," I said. "And Phil is fine too."

"I'm going to record the conference," she said, reaching for something on the bedside table. It was a microcassette recorder. "But you'd better take notes as well. You understand things better if you see them in writing. You'll have to sign a consent form."

"Phil is a full professor at the University of Washington now," I said. "He's researching orca migrations."

"Here's a clipping from the New York Times," she said, feeling around some more on the table. She held out a newspaper clipping. Her hand was shaking. I stared at the clipping but didn't take it. "It's about the procedure," she said. "Well, don't just sit there. When somebody hands you something, take it."

I took it.

She lay back against the pillows. I realized that she really needed a drink.

"So after you get your new liver," I said, "you won't drink again, right?"

"Do I pry into your private business?" she said.

"My liver is pretty damn private," I said.

"You would think I was asking for your life," she said.

"Not at all. You're only asking me to risk my life," I said. "I read about this operation on the plane. The donor doesn't always survive."

"Who gave you life in the first place?" she said. "Some women don't survive childbirth, but I took that risk for you."

"You took the risk for me? This is the first time I've heard that startling claim. You always said you had me to save your marriage."

"Do I have a marriage? Am I overlooking a husband somewhere in this room? You're the one who has a spectacular marriage to a spectacular man, which is all you can talk about. I stopped calling you years ago because I was sick of hearing about it. Do you know how vulgar it is to crow about something you've got to a person who longs for it but doesn't have it?"

"Maybe I should leave."

"Maybe you should. And when I'm dead you can gloat about how you let me die when you could have saved me." Tears of rage glistened in her sunken eyes.

"Get out of here. I knew I couldn't count on you." She turned her face away.

The day before the operation Phil flew in. "I hate my mother, but I don't want her to die," I said. "If she dies, the horror will go out of my life." I believe he would have stopped me if he could have, but he knew he couldn't, so he didn't put me through the ordeal of an argument. An hour before I was to be prepped, we both went in to see Ophelia.

A tight-lipped nurse with a covered bedpan was leaving as we walked in. Ophelia looked terrible. Her nose was red, and her hair was a mess. The room reeked of whiskey and vomit. I saw the empty pint bottle of Jim Beam in the wastebasket.

"One last binge," she slurred. "I'm getting a new liver, so what the hell?"

The veins stood out in Phil's neck, and his eyes threw out sparks. He looked at me but didn't say anything.

I wanted to strike Ophelia. "You are unreal," I said. "I'm not sure I'll have enough liver left over for the next donation. But that won't stop you from asking, will it?"

"Probably not," she said and lowered her scraggly lashes. "Don't you regret that you have only one liver to give for your mother?" She giggled.

I looked at Phil, and in his face I saw the limits of his patience. I had a terrible premonition that if I went through with this, even if I survived the operation, it would mean the end of our marriage.

I looked back at Ophelia. "You would ask me for my last drop of blood," I said, "and then when I gave it to you, you would say, 'That's not good enough.'"

"Well first, let's see how good your liver is," she said.

I was laughing so hard that I knocked a glass of water over and ruined the consent form. It tore when I tried to pick it up, and I had to ask the nurse to bring me another one.

# The Narrative Thread
## or Practice of Kanthas

*Andrena Zawinski*

*(Villanelle after the exhibition of quilts, The Narrative Thread: Contemporary Women's Embroidery in Rural India at The National Museum of Women in the Arts, Washington, D. C.)*

*(for Phoolan Devi, 1963-2001)*

They stitch as if we need these blankets to crawl under,
these thoughts that toss sweet dreams into fretful nights.
They stitch patches of stories onto a tongue of cloth.

They stitch–girls left to sicken, die, books torn from them–
stitch in women's fisted faces on a stammer of speech.
They stitch as if we need these blankets to crawl under.

They take to needle and thread in a revolution of stitch,
stitch speaking in streets without asking for permission.
They stitch patches of stories onto a tongue of cloth.

They stitch in women veiled at home, poisoned widows,
mango groves to chemical spills, wheatfields to AIDS.
They stitch as if we need these blankets to crawl under.

They stitch–girls burned by inlaws at husbands' pyres–
stitch palms ripe with fruit to gang rapes by authority.
They stitch patches of stories onto a tongue of cloth.

They stitch quilts for shoppers to slip under in dreams
 between borders stitched in a revolution of fingers.
They stitch as if we need these blankets to crawl under.
They stitch patches of stories onto a tongue of cloth.

◆►═◉═◄◆

*Author's Note:*
*In E. India, embroidering quilts (or kanthas given as gifts on fes-*
*tive occasions) depicting scenes from daily life (work, play, domes-*
*tic activity) dates back to the 18th Century. The craft disappeared*
*until the Adithi organization revived and transformed it into*
*grassroots activism in both its expression of social-political con-*
*cerns and as a source of income for housebound women in the low-*
*est caste. Phoolan Devi—a lower caste woman from N. India who*
*came to be known as the Bandit Queen and who was a victim of*
*multiple rapes, brutalization, then murder after her spree of vio-*
*lent vendettas—is idolized by many Indian women as a kind of*
*Robin Hood.*

# Husbandry

*Kyle Kuhn*

The wind blew snow across the fields, like mist curling off ocean billows, lifting the powder from the rooftops and making it sparkle in the moonlight. The gusts rushed through the timber north of the farm, shaking the blue spruces. Out of the milking barn window, Brent Vogul could see past his farm buildings and the folds of drifted snow to where the fields met the sky, but he couldn't see as far as the land he'd sold, ten of the acres his dad had signed over when he had retired. Selling the narrow piece of land along the St. Claire Creek, where Brent used to fish for crappie with his grandpa, was the only way he and his wife Emily could afford the in vitro. He still hadn't told his dad, and knowing how gossip traveled through the hills of Northeast Iowa, he would know within a matter of days.

An early December snowstorm rattled the walls. Winter had come on quickly, freezing the ground weeks before usual. During milking, the dairy cows wandered about the barn, looking weary from the cold. Exhausted, Brent opened the gate for the last pack of cows. As they flooded in, Emily appeared on the far end of the barn. She covered her face with her hand and leaned against the wall, her cheeks and eyes pale like the falling snow. Brent careened up the ramp through the cows.

"The test was negative," she said. The blue of her winter coat blurred in the dim light.

As he came toward her, he could see the darkness under her eyes and her pulled back mussy blonde hair. She stared off toward the empty milking stalls. She looked nothing like the woman he'd married five years before. When they had

met in college, her hair reminded him of the summer pra:
grass that grows in the waterways. She'd cut her hair sho1
few weeks ago, about the time she'd gone in to have the in
vitro egg transferred.

As he moved across the length of the barn, the cows
backed away and pushed against the steel barriers. "How
could that be?"

A few strands of loose hair lay stuck to her cheeks. He
put his arms around her, but she didn't move, feeling lifeless, like a sack of feed.

"I'm to blame," she said.

She smelled of vegetable oil and flour. He kissed her on
the neck. "It's not your fault."

"My body can't make a baby," she said.

"Don't talk like that."

When they were first married, the sight of the rolling
farmland had reminded him of the curves of Emily's body,
so that by the time he came in for supper he couldn't help
himself from making love to her. She had smelled like the
fields after rain and tasted of apple cider. Their bodies could
never be close enough. No matter how they wrapped their
arms and legs, he had wanted to feel more of her moist skin.
But five years of tests had drained her energy, and Brent had
to put up with her acting as if the marriage was a burden.
Now he felt none of the sexual desire.

"We can try again," he said.

"I'm sick of trying. I'm sick of the whole God damn
thing."

"It's not so bad."

She pushed him away and squinted. "How the hell can
you say that? You're not the one that had to go through all
the prodding."

Some of the cows had made their way into the milking
stalls while the others watched with wide, unblinking eyes,
looking worn out. Their hoofs clopped against the cement,
and they made huffing noises.

"You'll come around and want to try again. Take my word
for it," he said.

"Where're we going to find the money? You going to sell more land?"

He pictured the north ten he had sold, and the St. Claire snaking along the white field. "We'll find the money somewhere."

He reached out to hold her again, and she turned away. "This whole thing's been for nothing."

The hay and grain scent of manure came over him. "You act like you're the only one going through this."

Her cheeks turned a pinkish shade and she gave him a look as if she couldn't believe he had spoken those words. "Do you have any idea what it's like to know that your body can't make a baby?" She didn't wait for him to answer but left the barn.

When he came out to the drive, Emily was already inside the house. The beige paint had begun to peel, making the house look as if it were slowly falling to the soil. He'd meant to paint it the summer before. It never had looked neglected when his folks had lived there. He thought that maybe becoming a farmer had been a mistake.

The following morning Brent woke early to start chores. He drove the skid-loader, its headlights raking the darkness, carrying a hay bale toward the milking barn. The black and dingy-white Holsteins huddled in the waiting pen, hoof-deep in manure, steam pouring from their nostrils. They staggered up the ramp and into the barn.

His dad Walter had parked his truck in the drive. Going in through the tank building, thick with the warm smell of freshly collected milk, Brent found Walter in the barn, wearing a green DeKalb coat and a fluorescent orange stocking cap, watching the cows pour into the milking stalls.

"When do you put the feed out?" Walter asked.

"I do it after milking."

Walter had always come out ahead because, as he told Brent, he did things by the book. He used to say that if a farmer ain't honest then he ain't anything. When he had retired, and turned things over to Brent, he said he'd had all he could take of running the farm. Brent had thought this meant he trusted him to make his own decisions.

"You should put it out now," he said.

"I would if I had another man. It's just me this winter." Brent had laid-off his last hired hand a few weeks before because he could no longer afford him.

"Hire a man then."

Brent remembered standing in the barn, listening to his dad talk about farming - how planting too early in the spring would hurt the crop, how treating the cows cruelly would slow the milk production, and how taking on unnecessary expenses would cause foreclosure. Brent had been taught that the word "foreclosure" should be feared as much as "communism." Farming was Brent's future. Even at Iowa State, while he studied biology, it never occurred to him that he would do anything besides farm.

As the cows took their positions in the milking stalls, a heaving one with icicles hanging from her chin mounted another. The way her huge body quivered reminded Brent of the sex he'd had with Emily during the last few months. The heifer's back hooves slipped on the barn floor, and she fell off.

"This one's come around," Walter said.

Brent moved past him and patted the heifer on her side, whispering encouragement. She jerked forward and shoved into the group.

He went to the red case and took out the thin metal rod. He remembered the first time his dad had showed him how to do the insemination. Walter had said, "Now, a cow does her shitting and baby making out the same place. Humans got different pipes for those things." His way of teaching sex education. The procedure had been around for years before Walter had started using it. He had thought it was a waste of money, but his mind changed when neighboring farmers started getting better milk production from cows born through the process.

Placing the rod in the sperm receptacle, Brent pulled back

the plunger. He slipped the filled rod inside his coat to keep it warm and put on a plastic glove that reached his elbow.

Walter said, "I talked to Frank Sanderson out at his place today."

Brent rubbed the heifer's thigh. Then he reached his hand, wrist, and arm into her, warmth covering him, and dragged out the steaming shit. "What were you doing out there?"

"I was driving by his place and saw he had our north ten fenced off." Walter's voice rose like the tightening of a fiddle string. "So I went up and asked him about it. He told me you sold it to him last week."

Reaching in again, Brent pushed gently against the tender flesh and felt for the knot of the cervix. "I was getting around to telling you."

Walter took a few steps forward, lifting his stiff right leg out to the side. When Brent was a boy, his dad's walk had reminded him of John Wayne in the Rooster Cogburn movies. "You sold our north ten?"

The heifer began to stir, moving her hind legs. "We didn't have a choice. It's the only way we could pay for the in vitro."

Walter had a blank look with maybe the smallest glint of sympathy in his eyes. "If it ain't the Lord's will then it ain't going to happen."

Brent found the cervix and took the rod from his coat, slid it in, guiding it through the opening into the uterus. The cow bucked against the steel cage. He discharged the sperm and pulled the rod out.

"We've never sold an acre of this land," Walter said.

Brent slid his arm out and backed away from the cow. "Frank gave us a good price."

"I've been telling him we weren't interested in selling for the last twenty years. Then you go and sell it. Makes me look like a damn fool. But you're the fool. Why can't you two just let *nature* handle things?"

Brent laid the rod in the sink. As he took off the glove, the sight of his arm covered in cow shit made him unusually queasy. "We know what we're doing."

"This isn't just your farm," Walter said, almost whining. "It's Great Grandpa Sam's, Grandpa Gill's, and mine. You understand me?" He opened his arms as if he were Moses calling for God to part the Red Sea or maybe to strike down his son. Brent nodded. Walter left the barn.

Brent wanted to tell him that a baby could keep the marriage together and explain to him what it would mean to pass the farm onto a son. Someone to show how living off the land could mean everything, the way Walter had shown Brent. Raised to believe that the seasons, like everything about farming, were supposed to be predictable, he'd learned otherwise in his years as a husband and farm caretaker. His dad never had to decide between a child and the land.

The following day, he couldn't remember when the work had felt so lonely. The sounds of the farm, like the buzz of the generator and the bawling Holsteins, seemed more distinct. When he went to mix the morning batch of feed, one of the normal jobs of his old hired hand, Brent didn't add enough dry corn, throwing off the ratio. He barely started milking by the time they'd usually finished.

When he came in that evening, the only light on was in the bedroom. He ate the plate of food Emily had left for him in the refrigerator and then showered in the basement. When he came into the bedroom, covered only in a towel, Emily was wearing her white nightgown, reading a magazine on their bed.

She dropped the magazine into her lap. Her dark eyes looked middle-aged and her light complexion made her seem as if she were coming down with the flu. "Why don't we fuck," she said.

The room smelled of dry lilacs, and the lamp on the nightstand shed a warm glow over the bed. "You want me to talk dirty to you?" she asked. "Oh, Brent, I want to feel you inside me."

"What kind of talk is that?"

She pushed the magazine off the bed and it fell to the floor. "Let's *not* talk." She lifted her nightgown above her waist, revealing her blonde pubic hair, like a patient preparing for an examination. She leaned back on her elbows and sprawled out on the flowery bedspread.

"You know what I think," she said, her voice matter-of-fact. "I think the farm is to blame for all of this."

"The farm," he said.

She looked up, but rather than looking him in the eyes, she seemed to gaze at some place above him. "All the worrying about money and how we're going to make it. And selling that damn land."

"That's why we sold the land, Em," he said, raising his voice.

"Maybe if we had normal lives like the rest of the world..."

Suddenly he imagined himself, waiting helplessly for rain to fall, while he sat on his combine watching a thunderhead roll in from the west. "Nobody made you move to the country."

"What's that supposed to mean?" she asked.

"I didn't force you to be a farm wife."

Her face seemed to draw in, then something opened inside her, and she let out a breath from deep in her chest. "Why don't you just divorce me then? You can find a wife to give you a son. That's what you want."

He shed the towel and made a move toward the bed. She let herself fall back, her head sinking gently into the pillow. He covered and pushed himself inside her.

He felt her soft wetness from a distance, as if they were in a pornographic video. In the movies he'd seen in his college dorms, the performers' indifference showed through in their fake groans and orgasms. They talked of love as if it were something purchased on the home-shopping network. He didn't let himself think of Emily as his wife, as the carrier of his child, only a body below him made of flesh and skin.

The next morning, Brent returned to bed after milking, and then he awoke to the telephone ringing. Even before Emily had picked it up, he knew the call had something to do with his dad. He thought maybe he'd had a heart attack. He pushed himself up in bed, listening to her groggy voice. "Yes, I understand. I'll tell him." She put the receiver back in the cradle.

"Who was it?"

She rolled over onto her back and stared at the ceiling. "That was Frank Sanderson. Your dad's at his place. You're supposed to get out there."

Brent waited for her to finish. She pulled up the blankets and wrapped her arms against her chest. "That's all he told me."

Heavy snow fell as Brent spun out of the drive and onto the gravel road. The truck began to fishtail, but he didn't slow. The ditch might be better than whatever lay ahead. There was no telling with Walter. When Brent had played high school baseball, the umpires had thrown out Walter more than once. At bat, Brent had had difficulty concentrating on the pitches with his dad yelling from the bleachers. But now, Brent felt responsible. What if Walter had done something he couldn't take back?

He came over the last hill before the Sanderson acreage, which was tucked in the trees on the upslope. The narrow strip of land he'd sold ran lengthwise down the valley, glowing faintly in the morning sunlight. The new fence was a series of white posts strung together with wire.

Walter stood hunched, swaying back and forth over a post on the far end of the fence line. His green coat and fluorescent orange stocking cap stood out against the white hills surrounding him. Several posts lay scattered behind him.

The Sandersons looked on from their drive. Brent parked his truck and ran out to the field. The wind smelled dry and bit against his face as he high-stepped through the thick snow.

His lungs were burning by the time he neared the ravished fence. "Dad, what the hell are you doing?"

Walter looked up for a moment, then dug his feet into the snow and began to teeter again. He grunted as he lifted a post, threw it to the snow, and kicked the barbed wire aside. He breathed heavily and sweat ran down from underneath his stocking cap. "Frank wouldn't sell back the land. He said because of the fence. So I'm taking it down."

"You can't do that."

Walter dug his feet in and hugged another post. "It's our land."

Brent grabbed him by the shoulders and pulled him off the post. Walter stumbled backwards and caught his balance with his arms out.

"It isn't ours anymore," Brent said.

Walter bent over his knees, his eyes looked weary like that of an old bull. He seemed unaware of what he was doing. He dug in, then charged Brent as if he were the next post, swinging a right hook that grazed his shoulder. Walter fell to the snow, but got up and took another swing that hit Brent's chest, knocking the wind from him. Then he dove at his midsection, but Brent turned to his side and tossed him to the ground.

Walter lay there, his coat rising and falling with his breath. Brent readied himself for another pass, but he didn't move. He had a frightened look in his eyes. After Brent got his breath, he reached out to help him, but he swatted his hand away. Walter pushed himself to his feet and sauntered back toward the road, slumped over, his shoulders covered in snow. Brent followed, the taste of thick saliva in his mouth.

As they came to the trucks, Brent said, "I'm driving you home."

"I can drive myself."

Brent opened the passenger door, "Just get in."

He walked over to the house and apologized to the Sandersons. "I have to take the blame for this, Frank," he said. "I didn't tell him before we sold the land. I'll come by this afternoon and put the posts back up."

They drove silently past the countryside speckled with farmsteads. The wipers pushed snowflakes from the windshield. Walter looked out the window with his hands in his lap. His gloves, coat, and jeans were wet from the melted snow. Brent understood how desperation could fuel a man to pull posts from the frozen ground. It'd driven him to sell his family's land.

They drove through Clermont, the houses packed tightly like children's building blocks, and into the driveway of Walter's home. The forest green siding looked worn under the snow that had stacked in sheets on the overhangs.

"The doctor called the other day," Brent said. "Emily isn't pregnant."

Walter faced out toward his white yard.

"You know there isn't anything we can do about the land," Brent said. He felt a sinking in his gut, and he wanted to touch his dad, to pat him on the shoulder. "I shouldn't have sold it, but I don't want to hear any more."

They sat there a while as the snow fell gently to the truck. Then Walter opened his door. "You should try to get a hired-hand for milking. You don't want to wear yourself out going the winter alone."

He swung around and stepped down from the cab. The door shut gently, and he started toward the house. The flakes veiled his heavy body like a white silk drapery. He plodded through the snow, making two long tracks, yet he still walked with a slight hitch in his knee.

When Brent got back to the farm, he waited in his truck awhile. Snow had covered the rusted John Deere and filled the tractor's wheel wells. The cows bawled softly, the same sound that had lulled him to sleep after nightmares as a boy. In his mind's eye, he could see crowded fields of tall corn below a sky of hazy blue. Their leaves swayed and crackled in the wind. He could smell the earthy warm soil.

He went into the house. In the kitchen, the winter light came in through the windows, a shadow of the falling snow.

He found Emily curled up on the bed asleep with the bedspread pulled away. Her cheeks were flush, and he thought she might've been crying. She held her arms against her breasts and her straw-colored hair lay over her neck. Short breaths came from her slightly opened lips. The curve of her shoulders and hips reminded him of the hills again.

He sat on the edge of the bed. She had goose bumps, so he pulled up the bedspread and tucked it against her. Lying down, he kissed her lightly and wrapped his arms around her, feeling her chest fill with breath. For a moment, he thought about waking her to make love, but her warmth was enough.

79

# The Blue Butterflies

*Maurya Simon*

They swell into a kind of madness
against the rusted screen.
*Barbarians*, the children call them,
having learned this new word yesterday
while wandering through the library.
As the girls wave good-bye,
the first spring gusts lift their skirts
in waves; the school bell clangs.

Early in the early dark, dim blue squares
unhinge themselves, beating their wings
once more to get into the house.
It's like a clatter of breath, sadness
turned blue and lacy, the tiny stabs
of pain confounding the veins, nerves,
as blue snowflakes shower the mat.

Midnight and a single, spooled
filament articulates the world as,
unbidden, the moon offers its lamp.
Strange, these unrehearsed urges
to rise toward what's mysterious.
With deathly softness, a blue butterfly
flutters up into the star-cast nets.
Upstairs, one child cries out from sleep;
the other shields her eyes from the light.

# Split Second

*Manju Kak*

As I said, I opened the door and saw Anna crying. I mean what could have happened in that short time I spent at Tescos, me & the girls, filling up our trolleys with broccoli from Spain, cucumbers from France, zucchini from Italy, Jesus were there no British vegetables to be had in this European Union unless we bought them from that subversive grocer, the only true representative of the "islander at heart" on Marywynd Street? "Lassie you could try Lisbon for that English lettuce," he'd wink, "or come right here." Well, vegetables aside, Anna was crying and what could have happened between shopping and now? Hastily dropping bags, we were all over her; sweetheart, dahling, no no you mustn't, your mascara will... when she burst out, " But he's actually... dumped me." Just a second's silence, that split second of embarrassment, before the cooing resumed.

All we had heard about since we moved into the post-grad residence a couple of months ago was Stefan. Anna had spent the summer vacation with Stefan and he had shown her how to tie her shoelaces when rock climbing, taught her to fish. They had bought crabs, and he had shown her how to cook them, how to differentiate between the males and females, and about all the wonderful things a woman could do in a Norwegian village stretching through a sun encrusted summer when the boyfriend flies sea planes and between trips turns to her, her who has rushed to him during holidays filling the short summer with the glory of what happens when one is in love.

Anna, half-Arab, oldest, had been the envy of all of us four at the apartment: sharp shrewish Israeli Hillary (Media

Studies); bubbly nonsensical South African Margaret (Accounting); small stern German Ingrid (Linguistics); and I, come from India (Foreign Exchange), lost in this new Scottish landscape...I, who Anna (Design & Marketing) had first befriended when bereft of familiar surroundings and friends, I was unexpectedly homesick. It was Anna who had noticed it, who had understood rejection could come for any reason, short or fat, old or stupid, for colour or race, too, Anna of the dumping boy friend.

Stefan—who was tall, blonde, slim-waisted and lean-legged—did wonderful things when Anna of the dark long hair, lay back, perfumed, against eider pillows, mouth-washed with lingering fragrance, and waited.

Following that glorious summer when she returned to the apartment after classes, he called. Every other day *she* told us of the long delicious conversations, Stefan whispering beautiful things in her ear, after which her body tingled and glowed right into a morn of hastily pulled levis, rushed breakfast and the bus flagging routine to the Uni. Of all of us it was she who had it all: the rich father, the grades, the job to return to after the course, the blond boyfriend waiting at the end of each semester. But wait, here, now, she was crying, Anna crying for Stefan. Why did he no longer lust for her black lustrous locks, freshly washed?

Margaret carrying the heritage of those Dutch descendants pushed out, yes literally pushed out of new born Zimbabwe, stretched pale fingers from a pale blond body that had remained strangely fair in a hot country to stroke Anna's dark hair. In doing so they touched Ingrid's fingertips, strange quiet intense Ingrid, a hand that had that moment just left the comfortable pocket of her anorak. At the same moment, Hillary winced at Ingrid's first touch, her brown eyes carrying the heritage of the holocaust. At once came to Ingrid's own blue eyes the silent guilt of a third generation still bombarded by Bernard Levin's column in the Sunday Times, of un-enunciated German guilt. The innuendos of history that we carry on our backs, already hunched when we leave the womb, full of definition and metaphor at birth, that had kept the two of them cooking separate dinners from the common wired pool of starry tomatoes and oyster mushrooms, hate wallowing in Teflon between two girls, German and Jew, clad in jeans from Debenhams, the same Jigsaw T-shirts.

But that moment when epidermis touched epidermis, all melted for one split second in the common cauldron of a woman's hurt, for Anna was crying. Why had Stefan dumped her in the space of one full morning brightened by the yellow chrysanthemums she had bought just the other day standing yellow upon the windowsill, spilling upon the carpet. Why had he dumped her?

He says it will never work, she mumbled between tears. The seaplane job was suiting him fine and he didn't see why he should fly SAS again and live in so many strange hotels just to get a steady job, when the fishing in his home village of Sandanah was fine, and when from his house high on a mount he could see the blue fiords all day long. Yes why should he spend those glorious days in the cockpit of a commercial plane somewhere between Frankfurt and Dubai, when he could be home in Norway, flying the peripatetic plane. He did understand with his fishing, flying, house upon a hill, in a village near the sea, how could she, fashionable Anna bound for London, fit in. It wouldn't work he said, long phone calls that were expensive and weekends that just skied with the same regularity into his life. She a city girl needing to settle down, he a country boy wishing to roam? It never had.

We looked at each other. Now we could see his point of view very clearly, but could we accept it? It would be betrayal, would it not, and so in that split second that we had looked into each other's eyes, we looked away. Which of us could say to her, so he's right isn't he? Which of us could? German Ingrid, Rhodesian Margaret, Jewish Hillary, or I of India.

But before we could she saved us, "He's right, it really couldn't work." We boldly looked into each other's eyes, with the complicity of being the first to agree before we had been pre-empted. "He says he loves me still," she continued, "wants to come down and see me." Ah, the dumping became easier to bear, to console her with. So he loved her still, but since he was seeing how their relationship was going nowhere, leading to nothing, he was gentleman enough to warn her. That was not bad, not half that bad. "But I told him he shouldn't, there is no point, is there?" Anna's eyes upon us again. Was there any? Again looks exchanged but nothing given away before hand. "With exams coming up it would only upset me further." Yes, yes, we agreed rather hastily. We could not have her crying like this all over again. It seemed sensible to part now, after all he would just reiterate all he said over the phone, it was best left be.

Those finger tips began to withdraw, turn to bags of broccoli, cheese, milk, meats, each to separate continents withdrew, dinners to be cooked, assignments looked through. The crying had stopped, there was no more need.

But Anna sat on, I with her. Wasn't she the one who had first understood from me the rhythm of a rejected world? Now that world was she. When she spoke, it was as if from afar: "They are growing upon me, the years, are they not, I can see them." Discreetly from under my eyebrows I speculated; lines had come upon Anna's face, and her hips carried the weight of the chocolates she had consumed on her way to thirty-six. "Don't tell me they are not, don't deny," she burst out noisily. "Oo, there will be no man for me.... Never."

I couldn't leave her like that, a woman crying? I had to do something. Hastily I slipped into the common area. No one else was about. I took down her phone book, Stefan, Stefan, where are you Stefan... I had to tell him, someone had to tell him. There, under frequently used phone numbers he was. I dialed. The ring seemed to go on interminably. Finally it came. Ladbrokes, said the voice at the other end. Insurance Agents, can I help you ? After a split second I repeated, Stefan....? Stefan ? But there is no Stefan here, Madam. There never was a Stefan here. I'm afraid you have the wrong number.

⊷⊱◐ ◑⊰⊶

# Fishstalker

*Ivon B. Blum*

The light of a dull, workday morning creeps through the suburban bedroom window, which is nailed shut from the outside. The Navajo white walls look freshly painted, except where, in spite of repeated washing, the Rorschach patterns of food stains show. The sixty-watt overhead light, which is always on except when the bulb burns out, lights the bald head of the old man who sits, in tee shirt and pajama pants, perched on the edge of his worn recliner chair.

Hour after hour, the old man pumps his right arm from the ten o'clock position to the one o'clock position and back to the ten again. Casting his imaginary fly rod, he fishes strange rivers unconsciously revived from forgotten times far outside the barren room.

He sits perched on the edge of the recliner because of the times he'd leaned back too far by accident; and the quick snap of the chair frightened him; and he couldn't remember how to get back up.

It's better on the edge for fishing.

He perches there, as if on a steep riverbank, and casts the fly. His lips move constantly; but no sound comes out. He'd done all of the talking he would ever do to a wife who died and kids he does not now recognize and to judges, juries and clients in the long-ago courtrooms of his life before flame-out.

The old man is about to cast a generic nymph upstream when he hears a raspy lock-click. The door opens. A younger man, familiar looking, but always a stranger who comes every morning, enters, carrying a TV tray.

On the tray is a large plastic cup that says "Slurpy" on the side. The old man knows it contains water. Fishing can be thirsty work in the summers of the high mesa country. He looks for the baloney sandwich and it's there, too, although he seldom stops for lunch until the fishing slows in late afternoon.

Carefully, the younger man puts the TV tray down in front of the old man, just out of reach of the casting right arm.

"Here's your baloney sandwich, Dad, and water in case you get thirsty," the young man says.

The old man's son looks down on his father, tenderly remembering, as he always does in the fresh of the morning before the cares of the day.

"In the shower, I was thinking, Dad. Remember the time? No, you can't remember. Well, it was Halloween night. You took me to the local carnival at the shopping center. What was I then? Five? You took me into the maze. Held my hand tight. It was pitch black in there. I remember lots of people yelling and trampling around in the dark. My hand got jerked away from yours.

"I heard you yell for me. You made them turn on the lights; empty the maze—all the time yelling my name. But I'd found my own way out. I was watching the fun when you saw me and grabbed me up and hugged me."

The son tries to put a hand gently on his father's shoulder, but the old man pulls back like a snake ready to strike.

"And I remember I said, `Daddy, only little boys cry.'"

The son stops; swallows hard.

After a moment, he hears a horn honk.

"Gotta go, Dad. I'll leave the radio on so you can hear your jazz. Have a good day fishing."

The door closes with a whoosh and a slam. Miles Davis and "Sketches of Spain" trumpity-trumpet through the ceiling speakers. The old man completes the up-stream mend of his fly line. His lips pulse to the jazz rhythm, but no sound comes out.

"How's Dad?" says the son's wife as the son jumps into the car to get out of the heavy rain.

"Arm's going back and forth as usual."

"He just wades around in that la-la land of his," she says. "Like he'll - live forever!"

She starts the car.

"Seems like forever, sometimes," says the son. "I'm sorry."

"We're late to work. In this downpour, the freeway'll be jammed." The son's wife backs the car out into the steep-sloping street on the way to the cares of the day.

"You remember to lock his door?" she says.

"Sure. Yeah," says the son trying to remember.

The old man hears the car's tires squish on rain-soaked asphalt as it rolls down the long driveway and splashes through the trout stream of gutter-water.

It's raining, he thinks and pulls the rain hood of his wading jacket over his head. He looks up at the food-stained wall and sees a huge dam rising hundreds of feet above him as he fishes the tail-waters of a no-name river.

Ten o'clock to one o'clock, one o'clock to ten, single haul - and cast. Over and over again, his right arm ungulates to the rhythm of the background jazz. His lips pulse silently.

He fishes the rainy morning away; he changes flies; he lengthens his cast; he varies his drift; he watches the red yarn indicator bob again and again over the wind-ripply, dreamland river. But no fish takes the fly.

Sterile water, he thinks. Better move to faster water in this rain.

He gets up from his perch on the recliner. He stumbles against the TV tray and spills the Slurpy cup. Water splashes over the formless stains on the wall. His lips quiver faster, but without sound. He reaches for the door. It opens. He is not surprised.

Outdoors, he doesn't feel the wet or the cold as the rain

cascades off his smooth scalp to drench his tee shirt; for he has his rain hood pulled well over his head. The jacket covers the top of his chest-high, neoprene waders. The fast-running gutter-water swirls calf-high around his pajama leg and grabs a slipper from a bare foot. It rushes down the steeply sloping street. He feels the surge of the water but not the wet or the cold. His waders are insulated.

This is better, he thinks. Faster water will stir up more natural bait to keep my fly company. Surely, big trout are feeding in this run. Fishing is always better in the rain.

He wades swiftly in the downhill water of the gutter-river, wading faster and faster, always casting the fly: Ten o'clock to one o'clock, one o'clock to ten—

Suddenly, the pull of the gutter-river has him as it careens down the hill. It sucks the other slipper off, but he doesn't see the slipper disappear in the gutter-flood. He stumbles and grabs at his belt for the wading staff and pulls the string on his pajama pants. The slick river bottom of moss covered stones shifts under the weight of his felt soled wading boots. He stubs a bare toe on sharp concrete.

Well, I've been wet before, he thinks as he feels himself falling into the flow of the river. His left shoulder hits the street first, then his cheek. He doesn't feel pain; but feels the water rushing over him. He shoves the wading staff downstream and stops crossways of the gutter with his left arm pushed against the curb. Water rushes over his middle and tears at his loose pajama pants. The lips stampede, but without sound. Desperately, he hangs on to the fly rod.

He feels neighborly hands lift him.

Had a bit of a fall in the river, he thinks he says to the other fishermen who are helping him out of the fast run. Water came in my waders. Soaked my longjohns.

Nervously, he pulls at the loose pajama pants. Inside, he laughs to himself to cover the embarrassment.

Stubbed my boot on a slick rock, he thinks he says and thinks they hear him and excuse his clumsiness.

Then, he hears a siren. Out of the river! That's the signal! They're releasing water from the dam. That'll slow the fishing for sure. He thinks he shouts all this to the fishermen around him who are also rushing for the shore. His lips sputter gutter-water without sound.

On the shore he is placed on a stretcher. He hears the siren again and again. He thinks he calls out, "All clear."

His speechless lips tremble under the oxygen mask. Blood from his torn face stains the gutter-soaked tee shirt. Now he feels the pain a little.

I'll rest a while—till the all-clear stops.

The rain pounds the roof of the ambulance and its tires squish on wet asphalt. He hears the rain beating on the hood of his wading jacket, and he hears the siren, and he wants the baloney sandwich now that the fishing has slowed.

The sixty-watt overhead light, which is always on except when the bulb burns out, lights the bald head of the old man who sits perched on the edge of his worn recliner. A white bandage marks the left side of his wrinkled face. His right arm pulses up and down casting flies to saxophone rhythms.

The old man hears the raspy lock-click, sees the door swing open, smells the soup before he sees the TV tray enter the room.

The familiar-looking stranger puts the tray down in front of the recliner.

"Soup, Dad. Chicken. Not too hot. I tested it. You need to eat."

The son sees his father wrinkle his nose and frown.

"Keep an eye on him while he eats," the son hears his wife holler from the other room. "You know how he gets sometimes."

Then she looks in through the doorway.

"How're you feeling, Dad?" she says. "You really gave us a scare."

The old man's lips flutter without sound. The right arm casts the fly. Ten o'clock to one o'clock, one o'clock to ten, and . . . .

Suddenly, in mid-cast, the right arm stops. The left arm slashes across the TV tray and sends the soup bowl shattering against the wall.

"Damn it! Damn it!" the son's wife shouts and pummels tiny fists against her husband's back. The son grips the old man's arms. Still the right arm, although restricted, starts up again, pumping the fly. The lips flutter harder, the only sound escaping breath.

The wife sinks to the old man's bed and weeps.

"I can't stand it. He damn near died in the street in the rain. Now, again - this! It's him or me," she sobs.

Cold soup noodles slide down the wall to puddle on the floor. The son lets go of the old man. For a moment, the old man leans back in the recliner, but the chair does not snap him back. Almost instantly, the old man is again perched on the edge casting his flimsy arm and empty hand at the soup puddle on the floor by the wall.

"Now, dear," says the son. "He's just a very old man stalking ghost fish."

The son looks down at his father, remembering fishing with Dad in a lifetime of swift, deep waters, fishing that the old man has forgotten and the wife has never known.

"But, damn it. Don't you see?" his wife says.

The son looks over at her.

"What? See what?"

"Him. In his fishing la-la land. Escaping into the rain. Attacking the chicken soup. The mess. It never ends. Never."

The old man perches on the edge of his chair, his arm swinging past his daughter-in-law with the easy stroke of the headman's ax. Back and forth. Up and down—chopity-chop, chopity-chop.

The old man's silent lips flutter faster now.

The son sits on the bed beside his weeping wife and wraps an arm around her. He tries to smooth the pain-wrinkles from her face with a finger.

"I'm sorry," she whispers, sliding her head down on his chest.

"Me too, but—" the son pauses to smile at his father—
"you know what they say?"

"What?" she says.

"In the life of a man, God doesn't count a day spent fishing."

"Oh God!"

She looks up at him. Guilt? Fear? The son can't tell. He grins and dabs a tissue at her wet eyes.

"I'll get him some more soup," she says. The daughter-in-law gets up, tries not to look at the old man, can't help feeling the guillotine swing of the casting arm.

"I'll have to heat it again."

She moves toward the door.

"Not now, Honey," says the son. "Maybe later. Now, he's fishing."

The son gets up and follows his wife to the door.

"Does la-la land fishing count?" she asks her husband.

"Count?"

"In God's reckoning?"

"Oh. I don't know."

The son, still grinning, looks down at the old man.

"What do you think, Dad?"

His wife gives him a gentle punch on the arm.

"Well, at least this time - lock the door." Her soft whisper sounds like forgiving.

The old man hears the raspy lock-click. Jazz beats from the ceiling speakers. He looks up at the door, shades his eyes from the glare of the sixty-watt bulb and squints into the morning sunlight shining above the dam. He spots a buzzard circling down on him from rising thermals.

"What do you think, Dad?" he suddenly thinks he hears and looks all around the river, looking for a dad somewhere.

# Improvements

*Patricia Brodie*

*Breathe deeply.*

The oral surgeon adjusts the rubber cone.
Nitrous oxide flows.

*This will pinch.*

He injects my gums, my palate
with Novocain
shows me the titanium implant,
but I can't be bothered.
My mind drifts to our garden—
the old dogwood tree
too close to the house
had to be cut down.
The gardener is coming
to pull out the stump.

*Next, I'll do a bone graft,*
*mix silicone with your own powdered bone.*

When we moved here
that corner of the garden
had carnations,
azalea bushes, too.

There's the sound of the chain saw—
no, closer, close.

And why so hot?—
like our house in summer.

*A few stitches...*

At least we'll have air conditioning now.
They say the unit won't be too obvious
sitting on its cement slab
where the dogwood once flowered.

*and we're done.*
*Soon you won't notice the difference.*

# A Stump Ranch Chronicle

*Rae Ellen Lee*

"As soon as I light this fuse . . . " our father will say. And when he says that we know which stump we are supposed to hide behind.

My two little sisters and I crowd around my father, who is bent, shovel in hands, digging a hole under a big stump, one as wide as my father is tall. The early spring sun warms my shoulders as I rest my right hand lightly on the frayed hem of his gray jacket and listen to his breathing, louder now than usual. This stump is one of the biggest in the valley, this shallow dish of land we live on. The place is dotted with stumps, thousands of them, from trees cut before we bought the land a few years ago when I was little, the year I started grade school. Surrounding the valley on three sides is a steep, tree-covered slope. "The old river bank," our father has told us. I look in the direction of the Priest River, to where it now flows on the other side of the highway.

"You gotta give me some room, girls."

I drop my hand from my father's jacket, and my sisters and I step back as he reaches for the hatchet lying on the ground. A robin lands on a nearby stump, chirps, and flies away. My father chops a notch at the base of the stump. His loud breaths come more often. He drops the hatchet to the side of the stump, kneels, and pulls a stick of dynamite from his pack, along with a fuse and a cap. With a small tool he pokes a hole into the end of the dynamite. The fuse is about a foot long, and as big around as the veins on the back of my father's brown hands. He pushes the fuse into the cap and gently bites down to crimp them together. The two pieces now look like a metal firecracker with a very long fuse, and my father pushes the cap end of it into the hole he made in the stick of dynamite.

"There," he says, leaning against the stump. I know he is getting soot on his jacket. In one quick move, he takes off his stained gray hat, the one my mother says looks like the hat that Jimmy Stewart wore in a movie. He wipes his white forehead with his ragged sleeve, and when he puts his hat back on, all of his face is tan again. We watch his every move. He reaches his big left hand into his jacket pocket and pulls out a foil-covered pouch of tobacco, then pinches a gob of the stringy brown stuff between his thumb and finger. When he returns the pouch to his pocket, he brings out a tiny pack of cigarette papers. My father separates one paper from the others with his fingers and slips the pack back into his pocket. We watch him place the pinch of tobacco on the piece of paper, roll it up, lick along an edge, then strike a big wooden match up the side of his overalls, from his hip to his knee. He does this without thinking, it seems, and he's looking at nothing in particular while we watch him. The match pops and flares, and I wait for the odd smell I like. He takes a puff on his cigarette, inhaling deeply. Frogs are croaking, out in the middle of the valley. The wren sings, over by the pig shed on the slope below our house. Otherwise it is very quiet.

All summer long my sisters and I play hide and seek among the stumps and pick wild strawberries in the field beside them. We sit in the shade of the biggest ones while we eat the tiny sweet berries, and we try not to get soot on our clothes. On rainy days, in the house Daddy built us on the edge of the valley, I like to look out our picture window. I blur my eyes and instead of stumps I see a herd of friendly dark shapes, like buffaloes, grazing in our field.

"This stump's gonna blow sky high," Daddy says, exhaling. "We're gonna have to run for it."

My little sisters sit squatting, still watching him. Their eyes grow big. I'm ten. I'm their big sister, and I know we're safe if we're with our father, but they're younger, still little, and I'm not sure they know.

95

"Rae, you take Patsy's hand and run for your stump over there. Laurel, you come with me. And don't anyone come out from hiding until you hear me holler 'all clear.'"

"Okay, Daddy," I say. And I know he understands that he can count on me. He seems to know I'm big, that I'm responsible. I take Patsy's hand. She stands close and looks up at me. Daddy takes a final puff and stubs out his cigarette on the damp ground.

"As soon as I light this fuse . . . " He strikes another match on his pants, looks at each one of us, holds the match to the fuse, and says, "Now go!"

The stump I'm running for is another big one. Daddy stoops to pick up his pack and hatchet with one hand and takes Laurel's hand with the other. They aren't far away, and I can see that Daddy is only walking fast. He is taking long steps and hurrying, while Laurel trots along beside him. I slow down just for a second to look back at the stump. A trace of smoke is rising from the fuse as it burns toward the dynamite. When I turn back toward our hiding place, I suddenly trip and fall on my hands and knees in the wet, tan grass. Patsy stumbles, too, and lands beside me, screaming, "The stump! It's gonna fall on us!"

"Not if we hurry," I say. "Come on now." I scramble to my feet, pulling Patsy up by her arm. Daddy and Laurel have reached their stump. We run around behind our stump and huddle together. We wait. The fuse is still smoking. I look over toward my father and he nods to me. This is as good as a smile. I think about what will happen after the stump blows to pieces, about how we'll help Daddy make a pile of the pieces of wood so they can dry over the summer. Every spring we blow up about a dozen stumps, and we burn the piles in the fall. I do not ask my father how many years it will take to clear the valley. Finally we hear it—a loud boom. Patsy and I peek around our stump. Shielding our eyes with our hands, we both look way up into the watery blue sky. But it is lower down, just above the stump, that we see chunks of charred wood and pieces of stringy root, like big pieces of tobacco, shooting up no higher than our father is tall. When the pieces drop, dead, down around the stump, no one says a word. It's the same every time. I know he won't use enough dynamite to blow the stump sky high into small pieces that soar. And I know what will happen next. I know my father will say, "Should have used more dynamite." And I will wonder why he never does.

# December

*Jay Paul*

Dad brings her in shrieking, Aunt Kate, the night Ed is dead, her coat cloth and heavy and long, winter in her arms and face, her breath. And in the boots she kicks off in the hall to climb into the light, stocking feet on the waxed tiles. "Where is he?"—shrieking beneath the fluorescent light in Mom and Dad's gaze—"I want to see him. Where is he?"

The man born among the goats, he and his tall brothers, big gray-shirted men. Tallest on the teams in the old black-and-whites. Knot-knuckled, nicotine fingers. Who said *Dassn't* like a grinning conspiracy. The man with the birthmark escaping his thinning hair; and a bowed back, the price, he said, of blowing tenor sax.

His stories came out laughing. The bucket of milk propped over a door and his brother John guessing to go around, but not Pop, not Pop. The night the gristmill burned with Ed's car inside the garage, Ed riding the sleet-crusted hillside on the seat of his trousers. Spinning like a cartoon in his open jacket across the stream all ice the way wind ripples it. Getting there, to the flames running up walls and over the roof, in time, his coupe inside bright as day, paint and all, and patting a pocket for the keys, then another, another.

Story after story as though he had a big jar of them, like coins with strange faces and dates we'd love to have, screwed inside a careful top, the whole collection saved up.

And suddenly the season, two days before Christmas, is about taking, not giving and getting. It's about feet pressing on the banister railing through our socks, backs pressing the coldness out of the upstairs wall. About how hard my brother's bony shoulders sob against my skinny arm gone numb. And how many steps we'd have to dare to stride into that lower light where Aunt Kate is whimpering and Mom and Dad coax her to be quiet. Death is here, or has been, and left a body in pajamas and a bathrobe smelling over, the way an old man smells. Underneath one crutch, on top of another, at the foot of the stairs next door. Dropped but not forgotten. Death is someone who never forgets.

# Into the Box

*Kristin King*

Ten o'clock on a sweaty August night. The sun had gone down long ago, daylight giving way to a pitch black tempered only by the glare of the streetlights, and Stan stood in the kitchen, warming his wife's milk on the stove. Every night, she had to have steamed milk without the film on top; if he forgot about the film she would put the steamed milk down without drinking it and spend the night restlessly, sighing or kicking her legs around.

There were other things that his wife had to have. Stan always got home from his job as a manager at the train station at six o'clock, whereas she often got home from her accounting job at six forty-five. When Stan got home, the house was spotless because she woke every day at four to perform the exact same routine: sweep the kitchen and hallways; vacuum the living room and bedrooms; wipe off all the counters and sinks and spritz them with polish; dust under their wedding photographs; and do a number of other things Stan couldn't imagine needing to be done.

Sometimes she cleaned the same thing over twice, or three times, or five. Sometimes she was late to work because of all that cleaning. But if, at six forty-five, she came home and Stan had tracked in mud or spilled some marmalade on the kitchen floor, she would put her coat carefully in the closet, then sit down on the couch and cry.

Then, when Stan would get home from work the next night, there would be a note. "Darling," it would read, "Please be careful opening the refrigerator in case the ketchup falls. Thanks, turtledove. Patty." It was the one thing he couldn't stand, her calling him a turtledove when she was angry with him. All the rest of their marriage was perfect, but that one thing—well, it spoiled everything.

There wasn't any reason for it, but today when he had gotten home and noticed such a note sitting like a napkin in the napkin holder, his wedding ring had begun to turn cold, like a band of ice. He had tugged at it until his skin turned rough, then sat down and thought up the idea of the box.

When the milk was done, he poured it into her favorite mug, a tall one with a majestic handle, one she'd made herself in pottery class. He'd have to remember to break the handle off, later, to go into the box. While he was thinking of it, he wandered over to the refrigerator and snipped off the power cord, putting it on the counter. It would go into the box too.

"Here you go, Patty," he said when he brought the milk into her bedroom.

"Oh, thank you, honey," she said. She put her book down and looked up at him, dark circles under her eyes. "Aren't you coming to bed, sweet?"

"Oh, soon, soon," he said. "I've got work to do."

She sipped her milk. "Sleep well," she said.

"You too, honey," he said, and left the room.

It didn't take her long to fall asleep. Once he heard her slow, gentle snoring, he packed his suitcases and carried them out to the car. Even after all these years, there was not much he wanted to keep—his karate medals, his complete John Grisham set, his diplomas, and the model train (despite its smelling of Pledge). He finished well before midnight, when people were still driving around the city and getting drunk in the streets.

Then he got the box he'd found earlier that day, just the right size. He would keep it with him for a few weeks, a month, two months. Until she had found everything missing and given up, thrown her favorite things out. Then he'd mail it back.

Next he went through the house and removed the queen of spades from every deck of cards and put them in the box.

So much for her beating him at Hearts. He opened all the puzzles and removed one piece each. Into the box. From the Monopoly game, one property of each color. From Clue, Miss Scarlet with the candlestick in the conservatory. Into the box they went.

Then he sat at the table with a stack of books on one side and an Exacto knife on the other, and cut out the last page from every book. He put each book back on the bookshelf, exactly where it had been, then collected the papers in a neat stack and put a rubber band around them. Into the box.

Outside, everything was dark and quiet. Everyone slept now, dreamlessly. Stan took scissors and neatly snipped the buttons off all her dresses, jeans, slacks. He pulled one shoelace from each shoe. Into the box. He sawed off a quarter inch from one leg on each chair. He removed one shiny-clean knob each from everything: the TV, the stereo, the oven, the clock radio. Into the box.

Two in the morning. Now the dreams would start to come, and the guilty would have to face their secrets. Imaginary monsters would become real for those few hours of REM sleep. He removed the chain from the toilet, then wrapped it in a sandwich bag and carefully washed his hands. Into the box. All the reds from her oil paints, even though she no longer painted. The idle speed screw from her car. The power switch from her computer. A bulb from the flashlight, the hour hand from the clock, the cord from the phone, the screws from the frying pan handles. Into the box.

Three in the morning, the time the human spirit is at its lowest ebb, and he was almost done. He didn't know why, but he went into the bedroom and looked at her one last time. He leaned down to kiss her forehead, with the memory of her scent in his nose, impudent and tangy. But as he came nearer, he detected Pine Sol on her hands, and this gave him the strength to walk away without any kind of farewell.

On his way out of the bedroom he unplugged the control from the electric blanket. Into the box it went. The mug cowered on her nightstand, looking defenseless, and so he left the handle alone. He went out into the hall and closed the door.

He took the note and added it to the box. Then he taped the box together, stuck a mailing label on it, and printed her address, carefully, in thick black ink. It had to be sure to get there—that was the point. Get there in a month, too late. Then he put the box in his car, and then he drove away, his finger still cold. Dawn was breaking. Sun peeked in through the windows of what used to be his bedroom. His wife stirred.

# Strange Songs Beautifully

*Robin Reynolds Barre*

There is no animal with feathers
that is not a bird.
She sings what she hears.

Legs gaunt, no hallux, tarsus or wing bars,
she has not heard
there is no animal with feathers

that cannot fly. She hovers
over her range map. No words,
she sings what she hears:

redder, rare, river, rancor, and despair,
because birds live in this world.
There is no animal with feathers

that doesn't know the migrating weather
guiding the wired hand across the heart.
She sings, what she hears,

strange songs beautifully, and wonders
who will answer, who has heard.
There is no animal with feathers . . .
she only sings what she hears.

# Hallmark Cards

*JoAnn Kane*

Mitchell turned off the videotape, set his pencil down and grabbed the stack of mail I'd dropped on top of his manuscript paper. Unlike most composers, he thrived on interruptions:

"When I'm staring at a blank page, any intrusion into the thought process jolts the flow of creativity," he always claimed.

The first few months of our marriage, I had tiptoed around his studio, terrified of interrupting an Academy Award winning theme; but by our fourth year, I grew comfortable around his talent.

He sliced open a parchment envelope. "Nan, it's Larry's 70th birthday. Carla is giving a party at the Burton Club."

I stepped backward into his office and looked at him over my shoulder. "I take it we're invited?"

"Right. See what the calendar looks like October 12th. Is that a Saturday?"

I flipped to the next month. "It is. Are they dining and dancing?" I tried to look at the invitation.

Mitchell turned away to hide it, teasing: "Ooo. That should be interesting. Hmmm, I wonder who will be playing? I don't see anything about dancing, Nan."

"Let me see that." I swiped the invitation from him and searched for information. "A chamber concert and candlelight dinner? Wow! How formal. Do you think it will be black tie?"

"I doubt it. Carla is always specific about that. I'm sure it will just be fashionable."

"Guess I'll have to make a trip to Saks," I threatened. I paused in his doorway, "You RSVP, Mitch. They're your friends." Oh grief, I thought...another test. It's bad enough to attend these things and come up with clever things to say while sipping a drink, but what if I don't know anything about the music they're performing? I suppose I'll have to make some astute observation about the execution of it, while looking dazzling in some designer gown I don't yet own. I noticed the flowing crimson evening dress tempting me from the cover of Neimans. I loved being Mrs. Mitchell Layton but, with his life-experience, there was plenty to live up to.

By the time he was fifty, he'd scurried in and out of seven marriages, each of which he described to me like a narrator in a Neil Simon play. The shortest relationship, in time and height, was his third...a ninety-day whirl with a perky ice skater featured as the Mighty Montana Midget. He said it ended because he had no one to talk to. I didn't realize that was his sense of humor, so after our first date, I started to read *Time* and *The New Yorker* to keep up my side of the conversation. Whenever I met his friends, I figured they were wondering what he was doing with me. What I didn't know, was that they were wondering why I would take a chance on someone with Mitchell's past.

Labeled a child prodigy, he had rippled through Gershwin's *Rhapsody in Blue* with the Columbus Symphony at the age of twelve. By thirteen, he was playing a radio show four hours a day, fitting in a few morning classes at the junior high school. There wasn't much time for being a kid. "You're not going to play baseball! What if you break a finger?" his mother would scold. So he grew up running from piano competitions to recitals to the radio station. You might say Mitchell had always lived on the verge of a musical racetrack, spending years on the road...either in the band or leading the band.

His marriages began at eighteen. While playing the resort circuit, he met a long-legged, double-jointed twenty-eight year old dancer, billed as Holly. She was nuts about him, made him her love slave. He had the time of his young life. I imagine it was like having Anais Nin as an instructor with EROTICA as a textbook. As the summer season reached late August, Holly started planning their future. She had this gangster-type father who made sure she got anything she wanted, and she wanted the piano player. Her father had Mitchell picked up one morning and brought to city hall in Detroit. They were married by a superior court judge who was probably on the family payroll. Mitchell felt trapped and hated her for it. After that, he wouldn't touch her. She pouted. She cried. She screamed. She accused him of sleeping with her younger sister. He came home after a Saturday afternoon rehearsal to find her cutting up his clothes, tuxedo and all, with a single-edged razor blade. He escaped two days later by taking a job with a touring ice show. It took six months for the owner of the ice show to get him out of that marriage.

A more serious relationship developed over the next year with Karen, the star-skater of the show. This time, a judge in Milwaukee married them in spite of the objections of her umbilically-tied, stage mother, whom the judge nearly mistook for the bride. Eighteen months later, Mitchell found the threesome intolerable, but it took more than two years to extricate himself from that ice dance.

The Monday evening before the event, Mitchell asked me what I thought we could give Larry for his birthday.

"He's your friend and he's got everything. Why don't you ask Carla? Oh, I know. Remember how you loved the bottle of vintage port you got from your producer friend? Maybe you could find a seventy-five-year-old version.

"Brilliant, Nan! I'll call in the morning."

"I've got to find something to wear Saturday night," I announced as though it was an assignment.

"So why don't you go shopping?" Mitchell peered over the newspaper and his half rims, "Call that lady you like so much at Saks. I'm sure she'll have something for you to try."

"I just hate to spend the money."

"What?" he hollered. "Now you know that's not true. You just hate the whole process. And you never believe me when I tell you I like your outfit."

"I do too," I objected.

"Then why did you change clothes three times before we left for dinner last night? I told you I liked the first dress."

"Stop picking on me. I'm insecure," I pouted.

"Look Nan, I want you to feel good...God knows you look good in anything you put on...so go get something you like. Tomorrow."

Frustrated and tired, I drove out of the Saks parking lot toward home. There wasn't one elegant party dress in that whole department. Everything was either cut down to my navel or up to my stocking line. "What's the matter with these designers?" I complained to Yolanda, who always helped me. "Can't they package us in something pretty?" Worse, Mitchell would've had to pawn his 24-track mixing board to pay for one of those costumes. The price must be for the expert workmanship because it surely isn't the amount of yardage used. Besides, my spending all that money would be too reminiscent of his fourth wife.

Gena, a blond, curly-haired art student with expensive tastes and a passion for musicians, found Mitchell on the lower east side of New York impersonating one third of a jazz trio. It was a dark, red-leather boothed, smoky joint with gold framed oil paintings dressing the walls. Mitchell only played jazz if he was out of work because it wasn't his passion. He claimed that real jazz musicians were a different brand of performer, dedicated and devoted to that art form. Gena introduced him to the art forms of Rubens and Degas and together, between sets, they explored anatomy through the paintings of the Masters. A fine incentive for learning! They gazed at each other through periods of art history and by the time they reached impressionism, they'd decided to marry in the Monet garden at Tavern on the Green where they hired a small orchestra to play Delius's *Summer Nights on the River*. He was certain she was the right one. They were deliriously happy in their spendy, Soho loft where they entertained a variety of Gena's artist friends, none of whom were successful. On many evenings, the shabby group would run up Mitchell's tab at the club, sort of like Dorothy Parker's group at the Algonquin. This fourth union crumbled under mounting debts that demanded more in payments than a jazz musician could earn. Mitchell hit the musical road again, this time to accompany and conduct for Lorna, a really good jazz singer with a couple of hit records who paid well and was just too talented and cute to leave alone.

Three years and two European tours later, Lorna split to a detox center, divorced Mitchell and married her shrink. Back in New York at the Roxy, a calculating huntress, named Diana, was dancing circles around the newly-hired, musical director, Mitchell Layton, as he played and conducted three shows a night. A delightful flirt with sparkling black eyes and thick black hair laced in a French braid, she coaxed him to attend matinees at the ballet where instead of appreciating the art of the dance, he focused on exploring the scores of positions two bodies can assume. Diana was sleek and supple like a panther. She taught him how to slink across a dance floor to a tango; he taught her how to glide across his apartment floor into bed.

And so it went. Each new romance opened a door on more experiences to absorb, new horizons to explore. While other young men were attending college and humiliating themselves at frat house hazings, Mitchell was continuing his version of higher education by soaking up knowledge surrounding his relationships with women. He was busy being talented and becoming the brilliant, accomplished, seasoned, experienced guy I'd fall in love with. The one I'd have to worry and fret about, wondering whether I was even qualified to date him.

"Hello. This is Joan Cauldwell. May I speak to Mitchell?"

Every time Joan called she said exactly the same impersonal thing as if she assumed I was the secretary or housekeeper answering the phone.

"Oh, hi, Joan. It's Nan. How've you been?"

"Hello, Nan. I've just returned from New York. Where's Mitchell? Off recording?"

"No. Hold on. I'll get him."

She always spoke in compact sentences. No small talk, at least not with me. But of all Mitchell's wives, she had been the best influence on him. I'd considered sending Hallmark "thank you" cards to all of his lovelies, adding my own personal note of appreciation for that particular quality in my conglomerate soul mate for which each was responsible. Joan clearly deserved the biggest card for the best input. During her four year reign, he gave up the ivories for the pencil. He relocated to the west coast, advancing several rungs on the social ladder, hobnobbing with her friends. In order to survive in this echelon, he was forced to become a witty conversationalist or be stranded at the entry like a delivery boy while Hollywood hosts whisked Joan away to meet the latest so-and-so.

"Oh, Joan, dear, come with me. I want you to meet Anthony Drake of Lomans. I've told him all about your book and he's very interested in getting you on his lecture circuit." Clop, clop, clop, and she was gone. That happened to him once, and he swore it would never happen again. He said his whole life passed in front of him. He stood in an elevated, marble entryway alone, hoping and surveying the unfamiliar faces for a speck of warmth, but they were too busy enjoying his discomfort. They all just stared as though he'd been caught crashing the party.

Mitchell worked to fine-tune his manners and spiked them with a little "rude" to compete with the uppercrusties. He memorized jokes and retold them at the perfect moment with the timing of a comedian. After all, this snooty assemblage of humanity had a way of steamrollering anyone without credentials, unless one could dazzle them.

"What did Joan have to say?" I queried.

"She got the invitation to Larry's party. She was thinking of going and wondered if we'd be there."

"Why…so she can have Carla seat us next to her or across the room?" I snipped.

"Stop it, Nan. Joan really likes you and she wants us to meet her new friend, Robert. This could be serious between them. I think she wants us to make him feel comfortable at this little event; she certainly can't count on the rest of those nose-bleed types to give him a break."

"Sorry. She just seems so unapproachable to me, like she's always on a mission when she calls. Maybe next Saturday night we'll have a chance to talk."

Joan was a beauty: porcelain skin, light blond hair, dark green eyes. Though she was thin and only 5 feet 5 inches, she had a very long neck. She always looked striking in her marvelous wardrobe. Actresses and models seem to have remarkably long necks. It must be a prerequisite to being beautiful. I've never known anyone who is considered attractive whose head wasn't mounted high above her shoulders. Frankly, I don't even think one can pull off "haughty" without the E.T. look. The only downside comes with aging. As a person shrinks, that smooth, stretched skin comes cascading down, forming a terrace of folded flesh. Joan was holding up well. In her college days, she had studied communications at Stanford. She had a gift for getting information from people and used it to interview well-known artists and musicians for PBS specials.

The truth is, I'm puzzled why it didn't work out between Mitchell and her. Maybe I'll get some insight at this party...this test of my nerves. What if I embarrass him with a social blunder? "Oh, you're kidding. Finger bowl? It's so large I thought it was the soup course...or...I'm sorry, Mr. Mehta. Which orchestra did you say you conduct?"

Giving up on the ready-to-wear market, I flung open the louvered closet doors that revealed my less-than-stunning wardrobe and surveyed the possibilities. I noticed a bright green, linen/silk, jacquard print waistcoat adorning a simple black dress of the same luscious fabric. I'd purchased this Ungaro beauty several months ago when I got a call from Yolanda in designer clothes who'd put two dresses away for me to try when they'd gone on sale. After altering the length to fit my lanky frame, I bought it at a third of the original price. Now I had a chance to wear it. Mitchell would be so surprised.

Off we went to the affair...Mitchell in his gorgeous silk

burgundy coat and elegant black trousers and I in my opulent green jacket fastened by its ruby and rhinestone button over a tasteful black flared dress, black stockings and black cloth two-inch heels.

"You look smashing, Nan."

"And you look dashing, my love."

Even the parking attendants at the Burton Club were in fashionable, desert-red waist coats. I felt confident as we ascended, via elevator, to the third floor of this private retreat. We strode down the expansive yet sedate corridor toward the elaborately carved doors that concealed the walnut paneled library where the guests were assembled. I tried to make my neck a little longer by lowering my shoulders a bit.

Traffic had plotted to make us late, and I could hear the din of voices beyond...people engaged in the usual social balancing acts between drinks and hors d'oeuvres, conversation and gossip. The attendant pushed open both doors, allowing us to enter together. I watched a lot of heads turn to take note of our tardy entrance.

"Oh, no!" I gasped, choking on those words. This can't happen! Not tonight. Not at this party! There stood Joan in my dress.

A tiny size 4 version of my profusely green Ungaro creation stared back at me through the eye of that splendid button. You couldn't miss its brilliant hue, glowing amid the sea of black eveningwear that dominated the room. I desperately tried to shrink into my shoulders.

Fate had ordained me "twin for a night." I'll bet every woman here is roaring with laughter and thinking, "Thank God it's not me!" What I wouldn't give for Elizabeth Montgomery's nose. Oh Lord, what is Mitchell thinking? Does he see her? He must be stunned. He's definitely not laughing, or is he? If only it weren't bright green. I should have worn black. Why am I so tall? I must look like a Christmas decoration with my red face."

The dress was its own source of power, shining like a beacon. Poor Mitchell was once again on display in an elevated entryway. Before we moved to descend those two steps into the room, I glanced at him to see how he was surviving my first social crisis. He just winked at me and slid his arm around my waist, waved a big hello across the room to Larry and guided me right over to the designated green jacket area.

"Hello, you two," Joan smiled, completely unflustered. She turned to me, "Well, I see we both have the same exquisite taste in clothes, Nan."

She was perfect. She made me feel like nothing was amiss. "Thanks, Joan. I think we do it justice in both sizes."

"Absolutely," she agreed. "Now, Robert, this is my dear old friend, Mitchell and his gorgeous wife, Nan. This is my new friend, Robert Bennett."

Through the evening we endured many comments about our attire but the capper surfaced with a snide, "Did you girls go shopping together?"

Inspired by Joan's demeanor and wit, I replied with my most engaging smile, "No, but we intend to from now on."

Mitchell leaned over and whispered in my ear, "I'm crazy about you!"

# Song for a Ghost
# of Lake Drummond

*Renée Olander*

The landfill edges up against peat bog
and magnetic hot-spot—the so-called Great
Dismal Swamp, where snakes
still dangle from limbs along the shallow
crooked canal George Washington dug,
his compass tricked off-track. Here
black bears keep house
and a mercury-looking lake
laps shores where shells
tell ocean tales, and one can slip
in to skim some heat off summer.
Bald cypress knees and trunks
rise like knobby wisdom.
According to legend,
a native spirit lights her lamp
and roams some nights,
looking under the moon for her love.

A dark cusp of landfill liner
doesn't deter her. Wide-mouthed
moccasins glide among cypress,
bits of tackle and cloth, crackling plastic.
She doesn't find what she seeks.
She never does.
And the prehistoric lake lives
on high ground,

not far from where sludge
sucks amber sap and spits
certain alchemies back,
along shrunken edges of refuge,
lush as composted death.
When shadows fade into morning
motors, bug sprays, sodas,
floating lures and rubber boots,
not much marks her passage.

# Voyage of Discovery

*Barbara Whitby*

The university classroom has no windows, and the air is muggy from damp winter clothes. My attention periodically drifts away.

Out of the blue, I am riveted by what the professor is saying. He is inviting us to spend two weeks at sea on board a government research and survey vessel as part of the *Ecology and Resources* course. Those who choose to go will sail as "student scientists."

Never in my life have I dared to think of myself as a scientist. A few women braved the scientific world when I was growing up in the early 1930's, but my father was determined that I would not be among them. He strongly believed, like many other people at the time, that highly educated girls stood a poor chance of making a happy marriage. He also supported the medical hypothesis that it was dangerous to burden the brain of an adolescent female with academic study. Unlike a male's, a young woman's body, it was believed, was created for the primary purpose of childbearing. Too much stimulation of the brain might cause her to become sterile.

At this moment, when the professor includes me both as a bona fide scientit and as a peer with a generation, so much younger than myself (I returned to university to do postgraduate studies in my Senior years), I am brought unexpectedly face to face with my childhood past. I suddenly understand in a new way what it means to say, "I have come full circle."

I feel exhilarated.

To my surprise I am the only student in the class who wants to go. "It will be too dangerous so late in the year," someone says. "It is already well into October, and there have been several small ships lost in heavy storms in recent weeks." People nod agreement. Personally, however, I know that I don't have the same luxury of putting it off; it is now or never! The professor jots down my name and smiles as he says, "Welcome aboard!" The remark sounds very apropos, and I also take it to mean that he, at least, intends to sail with me, dangerous or not.

Ten days later I embark soon after sunrise. I note how rusty the old ship looks and wonder about safety. "Why didn't I have the sense to refuse?" I ask myself wryly. We have already been delayed because of a leak in the hull, and now there is some fault with the electrical system. We won't sail until dusk.

The four other students, each from a different university, are already drinking coffee in a small galley. The only female is from Edmonton. She is studying for a Masters degree, too, but in geology. She buttonholes me with tales of her work in mining camps up North, and I feel intimidated. There are also two women crew members and a palaeo-microbiologist; all the rest of the forty-or-so crew and the scientific team are men.

Our quarters are not at all the cramped accommodation I expected. As student scientists we have the benefits of officer status. I have a private cabin on the upper deck with a shower, a desk for my research, and two bunks. I opt for the top one. Through the porthole I can see high whitecaps, even though the glass is heavily crusted with salt. On a shelf in the locker are a hard hat and a life jacket. I put them both on and pose in outrageous attitudes, confirming my new image.

A notice hanging beside the bunks details what is unacceptable personal conduct on board. It makes me wonder what has gone on in the past, and I can't help hoping mischievously that this voyage will prove as exciting as these regulations subtly infer.

We are to eat formally in the officer's mess but at our own table. Our needs are to be taken care of by stewards, who will do innumerable tasks to ensure our comfort. I feel uncomfortably thrown back to childhood memories, to the heyday of British imperialism, which is exactly what I had wanted to leave behind me on this trip!

Still perceiving everything from an intellectual stance, I look around the lab where I will have various duties monitoring a number of scientific instruments. I must record their readings in a log every fifteen minutes. The equipment includes a sleevegun, a Klein sonar sidescan and Huntec sonar system. I have never seen anything like this before. The huge electrically-driven vibrocorer is stored on deck. It will be used for boring at great depth to retrieve samples from the ocean floor.

There are two more labs, where marine life and plants will be sorted after they have been dredged up in the grab bucket and preserved for further study ashore. Sand and rock samples will be evaluated for underwater mining potential. This shocks me. I have given little thought to the economic interests that drive the cruise. At present I am thinking only in an egocentric way. I feel extremely worried that I won't fulfill my responsibilities competently. At the same time, though, I am like a child let loose in an adult world—self important and engrossed almost entirely with the equipment and the performance expected of me.

At last we set sail! We leave the dock at that eerie, fleeting interval between sunset and nightfall. I feel between worlds, not quite detached from shore, not yet on the open sea. Small groups stand together on deck, lean over the rail, wing their goodbyes landwards. The lights of Halifax and Dartmouth, strung together by the thin outlines of the two bridges which join the cities across the harbour, look unearthly in the drifting mist.

Our first task also has an unearthly aspect. It is to review eighty or so mysterious circles that have been discovered on the muddy bottom at the mouth of Halifax harbour. They have caught the interest of UFO investigators, who have compared them with crop circles. We stare with awe at the sonar screen, and there they are, clearly depicted. "Are they the work of aliens, or the result of swirling ocean currents?" The leader of the survey team raised the question. I am impressed that he does not discount either theory out of hand.

My first night watch is behind me and I feel calmer, more comfortable with the technology. The openness with which we explored the circles seems to have profoundly altered my rationalist mindset. Now, at midnight, I squat alone, crouch in front of the mast, brace myself against the cold, as spray is cast rhythmically upwards by the wintry sea. I can't take my eyes off the moon. I peer skywards as well as I can through salt-spotted glasses.

"What is out there?" I shout into the wind. "What Worlds, what kinds of Beings above my head?" I stretch out my arms dramatically, daring 'them' to make themselves known, but I remain alone. It hasn't occurred to me to ask what is beneath my feet, although I relish the swell of the waves. As an Earth dweller, I am habitually attuned to the sky and to the near environment.

The second day out, excitement permeates the ship! The captain radioed the location of a suspicious looking package to the police, and it is discovered to be a stash of drugs. We are on the local news, still linked with urbanization.

Further out to sea we detect several wrecks, among them a large, unknown ocean liner lying on its side, its funnels clearly distinguishable. I never imagined that the sonar equipment would be so graphic . Was the ship torpedoed in World War II, and did it go down so quickly that all hands were lost before it could make its plight known?

It is flanked by shadowy areas, and one of the scientists identifies them for me as large schools of fish. I find it difficult to believe how distinctly I can track the soft bodies of small creatures fathoms below me. On the print-out it is clear that the sea floor is deeply scored by trawl lines. I feel emotional as I comprehend the extent of the destruction. Many species of fish lay their eggs among the rocks on the bottom, and it is obvious how much of their habitat has been devastated.

Paradoxically, through using the machine's eyes, my view of life is shifting. Subtly initiated into this technological world, senses I have never fully used become vibrantly present to me. Smell, sound, taste, touch and sight were always there for my use, but now for the first time I am keenly aware of what is above and below, as well as around me, and that I have a personal relationship with space. I never gave much thought to the life beneath my feet when I was on land, although I pride myself on my love of Nature. I certainly paid scant attention to the ocean depths except to be careful not to swim out too far. The profusion of life now seems to me to be magical.

This experience is intensified as we begin to use the "grab." When we haul the bucket back over the side, even the hardened scientists crane excitedly to look for new species of plants and marine life. For me, everything is new. I take a small mottled pink rock in my hands and stroke it wonderingly, thinking that it has been inaccessible to human touch before this moment. I remember my night on deck, shouting at the moon, thinking only of what existed above me. That we have raised this little rock up from fathoms underwater, to plunge it for the first time into air, makes the hairs bristle at the back of my neck as I connect the two occasions. I sadly watch the brilliance of its colour fade as it dries.

I try to share my reflections with one of the scientists, and he takes me back to a lab and spreads out several charts. "See these?" he asks, pointing out several areas on the map. "They were islands during the last Ice Age and were refuges for plants, animals and birds. The sea was much shallower, and the climate has fluctuated a great deal since. At present the water covers them, but who knows about the future?" Bringing over some sonar print-outs, he points out the evidence for ancient river beds and underwater mountains. "When you see this on your screen, and note that the water is getting shallower, you will have to hustle."

I find out what he means almost immediately during the

late night watch. A gale is heading our way, and we carefully monitor the three echo sounders and side scanners that are towed astern. We prepare to haul them on deck at short notice. They might hole the side in heavy seas. The ship plunges wildly; it is difficult to keep our feet. Suddenly the monitors show that the water is rapidly becoming shallower. What had been an intellectual exercise for me becomes vividly real, as I recognize the signs that an undersea hillside is looming up fast. We race on deck to rescue the equipment, fighting desperately with the wind.

We run before the violence of the gale, seeking safe harbour in Chedabucto Bay. I cling to my bunk. Suddenly the cabin seems transformed. It appears as a true shelter, not necessarily from danger, but in identifying for me that I am not separable from the elements. The noise is deafening, the plunging of the ship alarming, and the waves outside my porthole look gigantic, but they no longer appear 'outside' the porthole. I am not the detached observer I was when I came aboard. I could not now look up at the moon as a separate sphere in the way I did that first night. I am conscious, all the time, of what is above, below, around and within me. At some time during this voyage, and I cannot say when, I moved away from the role of student scientist. I feel an integrity, a keener awareness of what I share with all other forms of life. In a strange manner technology enlivened and enabled me, but I don't think that would have happened in the same way if I had not also been out of my usual environment.

A shape flashes past the porthole, and then another. A flock of seagulls is following the ship but not alighting. They are a brilliant emerald, the light thrown up from the water transforms their plumage. They skim the waves, frolic in the wind, dive for fish. They look mystical, figuratively joining the sky, the surface and the life beneath...as my eyes trace their circuit, I too take flight.

# Crossing Cold Water:
## Voyages to the Last Frontier
*Rebecca Goodrich*

### I.

The sharp prow of our skiff cuts through green water like a knife, peeling back a perfect curl of white that gradually dissolves into a widening V. We pound across the corrugated chop, foot-high waves lifted by the friction of wind, each edged with a ruffle of foam like windblown lace. A low ceiling of gunmetal gray stretches to the ragged horizon. My left hand grasps the lip of the wooden seat beneath me; I latch myself tight like a limpet or whelk on a storm-beaten beach. My other arm encircles the life-jacketed two-year-old on my lap, a living seat belt to keep her from flying out of the boat with each jarring thump. At my side her sister, four, hangs on with one arm looped around my elbow, the other grasping the seat as I do. Black plastic garbage bags stuffed with clean laundry and taped cardboard boxes of groceries crowd our booted feet. My husband stands tall in the stern, the outboard tiller tilted to reach his gloved hand; he takes each blast of spray in the face, eyes narrowed, looking for the bobbing log, the tossed flotsam, the black rocks barely submerged by the high tide. The children and I face the stern, watching the lights of town recede to glowing pinpoints in the murk.

### II.

The sun sets in vermilion; on the water a wavering red road leads to a spot where the sun balances on the flat edge of space. Two eagles approach each other, then collide with a sound like bones striking sand. Their talons interlock with an audible clack and they rock apart, a feathered mandala reeling toward red water. Tumbling in slow time, do they know how quickly the flat, glassy plane rushes toward them? A moment before they plunge into the sun's reflection they part in a perfect double parabola and rocket upward.

### III.

On winter afternoons the cabin grows dim too early. We light three kerosene lamps around 3:00. Their glow is yellow; the light flickers and jumps on plywood walls. To read I hold a book a foot away from the glass chimney so the light falls full on the page. Even so my eyes strain. Sometimes this light is not enough. We grow irritable, angry, pressed and weighted by the dark till a tickle of panic flutters in our throats. My husband goes outside and I hear the rattle of the starter cord and in a minute the Honda generator revs and the overhead bulbs in their porcelain sockets blaze. The light is so bright it hurts. We soak up incandescence like sunbathers. But each minute of light is money spent for fuel, so soon the generator is extinguished and we head for bed.

### IV.

Our highway home is a blue channel that winds between steep forested slopes. On windless days we nearly fly over glass-smooth seas, but today the trip will be long and exhausting as we fight the invisible resistance of wind. Our rubber raincoats rattle and jerk, plucked at by thin fingers of moving air. The skiff powers up and over each crest, then falls into each trough with a rivet-battering bang. Pellets of rain tap at my hood: an insistent *pit, pit, pit* that calls me out of myself. My focus becomes dislocated; the world becomes a small, wavering watercolor of azure, verdure, gray. I inhabit only this jarring, buffeted, wet moment in a metal boat on wild green water.

V.

Rain washes the rectangular metal roof and collects in plastic gutters angled toward the downspouts. Pipes connected to each other by silver Duct tape carry it to the square plastic ice tote at the southeast corner of the house. *Ice tote* because it is the same square plastic container, four feet deep and wide, that the canneries use to store fresh fish and chipped ice: to wheel about on roaring forklifts, from the dock, to the slime line, then the blast freezer. It is white, translucent, like the ice it was intended for. Now it collects rain for washing. I climb on a stump for leverage and dip a five-gallon bucketful, lifting with my back and shoulders and legs. I will heat the rain in a black enamel canner on the propane stove till it boils, then use it to wash and rinse the dishes. To bathe, we will arrange buckets of cold rain in a row by the tub and add boiling rain to each till they're tepid. The bather stands naked while another pours rain from a bucket over the head, the back. A quick lather, a shampoo, then a rinse. As we towel off by the woodstove we pluck hemlock needles from our wet hair.

VI.

The island is heavily wooded but firewood comes from the ocean. Huge rafts of logs ply the channel, towed by ocean-going tugs, bound for the sulphur-spewing pulp mill up a narrow bay to the east. Logs break away and litter the beaches up and down the coast. Some are straight-grained, long and limbless, collected by thrifty builders and sawn into green lumber at small, portable beach mills powered by Volkswagen engines. The tide delivers one to our front door, and I learn to use a chainsaw. My husband is away; I am alone on the island except for two napping girls. The starter cord snaps like a whip, wound on a tight spring. The engine roars to life and I make the blades whiz with my trigger finger. I am tentative at first; the chain bites into wood and a satisfying shower of fragrant dust flies over my shoulder. One slab falls away, round and golden as a biscuit. But what would happen if this thing bucks or the spinning chain bites my bone instead of wood? A moment before I felt heroic, now I feel mortal. I turn off the machine and go to make sure the children are still breathing.

## VII.

Hemlocks and yellow cedar grow knurled on rocky outcroppings. Their outer limbs hang into the spray zone, stunted by sharp, prevailing winds and mere inches of top-soil. I find two, growing side by side on a boulder. They are ageless. Their roots are half exposed, washed clean by a churning high tide. Each reaches out with a twisted limb that curls around the trunk of the other so that they stand in that place, facing the ocean, embracing like old friends.

## VIII.

We've dallied in town and now it's night. We motor around the rocky breakwater and enter into darkness so thick I fancy I could heft it, gather a fistful. There is no wind and the water undulates around us flat and black as oil. It shivers like a muscled hide, rolls away from the bow in a smooth curve like the flank of a whale. If we look behind us the lights of town make wavering paths on the dark water, like tapers lit for prayer. Ahead, the night is heavy, complete. Halfway home we kill the engine, the skiff slows and settles. We rock in the swell, pressed on all sides by the absence of light. Pebbles on a near shore rattle in the surf. Small waves slap with a sound like bare hands clapping. A bell buoy tolls, chiming twice with each surge. My senses expand like ripples on a pond, penumbral forms take shape: a low wooded island to port, a floating log off the bow, barely submerged boulders nearby. With lightless precision we echolocate north, east, south, west. The starter cord snaps, the outboard comes alive, we glide the rest of the way home, seeing with blind eyes.

## IX.

Rubber tires make garden boxes on this cobbled beach. I arrange six and fill them with the red volcanic ash that passes for topsoil here. A bag of peat to temper the sandy ash and I'm ready to plant: lettuce, radish, marigolds. Green sprigs emerge under sky the color of skim milk. The slips are watered daily, automatically, when the clouds that roil in from the Pacific snag on the jagged peaks to the north. Then one day they are gone, mowed down, grazed away. Slugs, I am told, and go on the warpath. The girls and I collect slugs in a bucket each morning, six shining inches long, curled on spongy beds of damp moss or lounging under dripping leaves of blueberry and false azalea. We march down the boulder-strewn beach to the low-tide zone where pools have formed in crevices and depressions. Crusty orange and purple starfish cling to the rocks in tangled clusters. In permanent pools, barnacles wave at us with feathered feet, inch-long sculpins the color of sand dart from wall to wall, and bouquets of sea anemones bloom from squat, fleshy stalks. Some look like white broccoli flowerets, others sprout pale pink tentacles from a thick stem of mottled red and olive. Into each we drop a live slug and watch the tendrils slowly curl. Sometimes one bubble of air escapes from the mouth of the doomed slug as the hundred wavering arms embrace it. After a year of feeding these living flowers, people comment on the extraordinary beauty of the tide pools on our side of the island.

X.

Beneath our flying hull is a topography as rugged and eroded as the forested slopes that rise to crags in the distance. Beneath this tarnished silver surface: cobbled slopes encrusted with pink sponge and scuttling crabs, an ancient canyon that once ran with meltwater from snowfields whose steep bouldered walls now hide eels and rockfish, deep graveled stretches where halibut forage. Prehistoric campsites on submerged beaches, middens filled with bones and shells. Rivers within seawater, cooler currents flowing below light-warmed layers in silent, submerged waves. Clouds of krill and herring. Salmon, lingcod, porpoise, and whales winging through black water beneath us.

## XI.

I hear a hard thump on the roof and run out the door to investigate. On the back porch a nice, twelve-inch Dolly Varden trout shivers and flops. I look up and see a large eagle perched on an overhanging limb. *Thank you*, I shout, then call the little girls to show them. Together we slit the belly and find a handful of thin, silvery needlefish. *The trout eats the needlefish, we eat the trout.* They watch with eyes wide and knowing. After I wrap the fish carefully and put it away for dinner - another thud. Another fish, this one larger and fatter than the last. The eagle nods and bobs on the thin limb. Years later I tell a Yu'pik friend about the fish and the eagle. *Those fish were a gift you know*, she said. I knew it then, because they tasted so good.

## XII.

When we reach the protected cove we execute a critically timed maneuver we've perfected to beach the skiff, unload children, groceries, water jugs, and laundry. Like choreographed dancers we rush the pebbled shore, grinding the bow into a section of gravel between black, basalt boulders. I'm mounted in the bow like a figurehead, and at the moment of contact I vault over the side into the surf and pull the skiff forward another foot. Timing our passes with the surge, we hand over the plastic sacks that hold supplies from town, the little girls, the red plastic Jeri jugs of drinking water we filled at the harbor tap. Sometimes a wave rolls in and over the top of my boots. The chill is electric.

## XIII.

In the center of the harbor is a huge boulder with a smooth, rounded crown. At high tides inrushing waves pour over its top like molten glass; at low tides it parts the water into twin swirling vortexes that curl around its base. At its apex is a rounded depression like a polished bowl where water settles between tides, reflecting the changing sky like a skrying mirror. Beside the bowl of water is a burnished bronze staple. It is thick as a child's wrist, bent into an arc

127

and pounded into the solid rock by Russians one hundred and fifty years ago. They named this island *Bamdoroshni*, logged it thoroughly, used the staple on the rock to keep their rafts of wood from floating off. The staple and the rock seem to have melded, their molecules so mingled and grown together that it's difficult to tell where the bronze ends and the basalt begins.

### XIV.

On Thanksgiving Day the wind blows fifty knots. Waves like green walls rise and speed toward our beach where they crash with a sound like a train wreck. The tide is the highest of the year and each exploding wave reaches a little farther toward the cabin. Soon spray pellets the windows. Tree limbs whip wildly, flinging twigs and cones like shrapnel. Behind the house a peeling whine so loud it sets my teeth on edge. We rush to the back porch in time to see a giant spruce up-end and fall, its flat platter of roots lifting a ton of forest floor, leaving a divot twelve feet wide and five feet deep. Back inside we sit to eat, watching the clock for the moment when the tide will turn and begin its slow, incremental retreat. I look outside and then look twice; a man is rowing by in a wooden dory, the kind of heavy double-ender that whalers fished from a century ago. It occurs to me I may be seeing a ghost, a phantom from the early halibut dory fleet that fished exactly where he rows. But then he sees us framed in the window and lifts his head in acknowledgement. He strains against the wind, up and over an incoming wave and then disappears from view.

# On Rain

*Susan Zwinger*

Thank God for this rain. For this silver scribble
against all that is dark. For its sonorous sizzle on top of tar
roof and parking lot. For this barometric tragedy,
for this drab flab of sky. Thank God for a perturbed
stench of air and molding soil, for adolescent boys
who go by in a mob, for robins
whose song is silenced by rain.
For fat, slovenly drops which keep Californians
from our shores. Thank God for death, which keeps us
from stacking like cords. For loss and for pain,
which fills the nightclubs with smoky ululation.
Thank God for the taste of rain on our tongues,
for its feel on our faces washing away conceit. For its distant
frying sound mistaken for surf or French fried
potatoes in grease, for sheets of airborne sea.
Thank God that we can bury grief in work or ice cream
or atrocious TV. Thank God for my blank vaults of brain.
Thank God for rain.

# The Men You Don't Get to Sleep With

*Susan Rich*

Are always the men that you want;
the ones who hide something

in their long-fingered hands
and won't let you touch it or tap it;

who refuse your good offerings
of dark chocolate and flan;

the men who come quoting
Keats, who winter in Cannes,

who summit Rainier
without ropes or brains.

These fleeting men; fantasies
we hold for years past their time,

one lone kiss from a cabinet maker,
all night laughter with a Bosnian

jailer, the amaranth flavor
of a passionate painter. No,

that's not it, it's not what you think.
Not needing that stick but the act

of his tongue licking crumbs, soft
breath in your ear as he offers gently

*This is actually fun.*
Caleb, Dan, the photographer man;

the ones with crushed hearts
and the ones who had none.

Damn these men, remembered
unnaturally long; did their bodies

shelter something lacquered and spun,
something even today, you wish that

you'd won? But what if sexual
climax was reached with the barista,

the sculptor, the sheik? What then?
Then what would we do?

The riddle undressed, the pleasure
no more than ho-hum.

Better to keep imagining this:
an allusive rhyme, enhanced and revised

on mountain paths, window seats,
private jets, the men that you don't get

you do get: set in pen and ink,
fantasy and less grief

they can unceasingly please.

# Uncle Fred and the Sound of One Hand Clapping
*Wayne Ude*

My uncle Fred is an extremely stubborn one-armed farmer. He didn't start out one-armed—that was one of the side effects of farming—and he wasn't supposed to be a farmer, but to inherit his father's bank. He might have, too, if the old man hadn't forbidden him to try farming first. Once Fred was faced with the ultimatum, he became a farmer, eventually one-armed, who developed an obsessive interest in the inner workings of human beings, which doesn't mean what you may think. From about the age of forty on, Uncle Fred wanted to be both a one-armed farmer and a proctologist.

There was no medical school in the state, so Fred studied proctology on his own, the same way he'd learned to overhaul his combine. First he read some books, and when he figured he was as ready as he was ever going to be, he rented an office, hired a nurse/receptionist, bought some equipment including an evil-looking rectal periscope, and opened for business.

Fred didn't get many customers, of course. Who wanders off the street into a proctologist's office? "I've been meaning to have someone take a good look up there anyway, so I guess I might as well get it done now while I've got a few minutes." Like other specialists, proctologists rely on other doctors to refer patients, and the only doctor in town who knew Uncle Fred was the surgeon who'd amputated that left arm after its complicated encounter with a silage auger. That doctor wasn't about to refer patients to a farmer who hadn't even been able to keep his own limbs intact.

Still, a couple of patients did show up. The first was sent by a very young and naïve doctor, new in town and still ostracized by the established medicos who resented his competition almost as much as they did his up-to-date competence; the second came from one of the medical alcoholics who no longer always knew just what he was doing. The young doctor sent three more and the alky one before the state Medical Society noticed Uncle Fred and shut him down, despite Fred's success: Looking into a patient with his rectal periscope, Uncle Fred had found the beginnings of a tumor early enough for it to be easily and safely removed.

Farmers are stubborn people—otherwise, they'd put that energy and initiative into something that makes real money—and Uncle Fred would have been stubborn even if he'd gone into his father's banking business instead of becoming a farmer. Being shut down and threatened with prison only delayed Fred's proctology practice long enough for him to find a correspondence diploma mill. In a few months the office was open again—new location, different nurse, same evil-looking rectal periscope that had already saved one life, framed diplomas on the walls and on the new resume Uncle Fred sent around to all the doctors in town.

This time the Medical Society didn't get around to checking Fred's credentials for almost a year, during which time he'd diagnosed two or three serious problems in the early stages, according to the doctors who'd sent him patients this time around—the young one and two relatively sober others, the alky having been forced into retirement by a series of malpractice losses and the cancellation of his insurance. Without Uncle Fred, the nearest proctologist was a hundred miles away, so Fred's proximity made the locals a little more willing to order tests they might otherwise have skipped or put off for a while.

Of course, the Medical Society shut Fred down once more. This time they really got his dander up, threatening prosecution if he did any more sight-seeing by periscope. For

Fred, that meant it was time to get himself down to one of those barely-accredited Caribbean medical schools. He rented out the farm for three years and, in my Aunt Thelma's words, forced her to go along to the Virgin Islands and do nothing but lie out on beaches, learn to scuba dive, and fight sunburn when she wasn't helping Fred with his homework and learning Caribbean cooking.

When he put up his shingle this time around, there wasn't much the Medical Society could do about Fred's office being open (by appointment only) on Mondays and Tuesdays. He farmed Wednesday through Saturday, but like most farmers, he made Saturday into a half-day whenever the work load wasn't too great and worked around the clock seven days a week when he had to. During irrigation and harvest seasons Fred would shut the office down for a couple of weeks. As he put it, after a week of irrigating around the clock he was so groggy he'd be apt to see little green men through that periscope anyway.

It was during the slow season that I dropped by on my way home from college and, as usual, made sure I arrived about dinnertime on Saturday. Now I want to make it clear that I'd had nothing to do with Fred becoming a farmer or a one-armed farmer or a proctologist. But I do bear some responsibility for the Center for the Study of Zen that's now located next to his proctology office.

When I arrived, Thelma was in the kitchen fixing a feast. I wasn't sure, but it looked like a whole pig might be rotating on the spit in the glassed-in indoor electric roasting fireplace she'd insisted on when they got back from the Caribbean. The only real problem with visiting those two was that I might be too full afterwards to drive the last hour home without a nap first. We chatted for a while and looked at the latest set of pictures from Caribbean friends before she told me to get out of the way and let her finish dinner. I gave her a kiss, which always seemed to fluster Thelma, and wandered out to the barn to visit with Uncle Fred for a while before we got called in.

I was full of new things I'd learned at college and Uncle

Fred would want to hear all about them. I especially wanted to tell him about my discovery of Zen Buddhism and koans—those enigmatic sayings whose resolution is the key to enlightenment. My exploration so far had consisted of after-midnight conversations with a fellow sophomore who claimed to be a Buddhist and—as I learned later—was mainly quoting from a big book of koans he'd found in the college bookstore. So I didn't have any idea about the answers to any koans or just what enlightenment was, but I could hardly wait to tell Fred all about them anyway.

I found Uncle Fred sitting on a hay bale in the barn—Fred kept a couple of cows for beef and a couple of pigs as well, and Thelma had some chickens and a couple of turkeys. Mostly he grew a lot of alfalfa, some wheat, a fair amount of barley and oats, and he always had some hay bales around to sit on. I'm not sure whether he was actually doing anything at the moment; he may have been just thinking and waiting for Thelma to call dinner, or maybe even waiting for me.

Uncle Fred waved me to a hay bale and asked me if I'd learned anything that quarter. I started in about Zen, and Fred listened, nodding from time to time to let me know he was following. I told him about the priest who had studied for years and years, but enlightenment just didn't come until one day his master pointed out a tiny wildflower in the grass and said it had a wondrous smell. When the student bent to experience the smell for himself, the master stepped back, got a good run, and kicked the apprentice so hard he left the ground and came down on his face a few feet further on—and by the time that apprentice landed, he was laughing with the joy of enlightenment, which had entered at the moment of supreme astonishment at being kicked by his Master while his nostrils were still full of the scent of that tiny flower. Fred laughed at that and said he'd always thought a good kick in the ass would do most students a lot of good.

And then, instead of leaving well enough alone, I had to let my mouth carry me where I shouldn't have gone:

"They have these great little sayings called koans"—I pronounced it "cone" and still don't know if that's anywhere near correct or not—"that at first don't make sense in the regular way, but then they suddenly do and the whole universe comes clear at once!"

"Kind of like a swift kick in the ass?" Fred asked.

"Right! A spiritual kick in the ass!"

We both laughed for a moment, and then Fred said, "So let's hear one. I haven't had a good spiritual kick in the ass in years."

Well, the koan that came to mind was the most famous of all, and I blurted it without thinking: "What is the sound of one hand clapping?"—realized what I'd said, and waited in shame and horror for my one-armed uncle's reaction.

Fred sat calmly, thinking for a moment, then gestured me closer. I leaned forward; he spoke softly. "I think I know the answer." He beckoned me just a little closer still, and as I leaned in expectantly, he swung that one good arm, palm cupped, so hard against the left side of my head I nearly fell off my hay bale.

My ear rang so loudly that I could hardly hear my one-armed uncle as he said, barely getting the words out through his own laughter "There! Do you hear it? The sound of one hand clapping! Have I enlightened you?"

And do you know, I realized, as I joined in his laughter, that once more Uncle Fred had gotten it exactly right. Six months later, Fred rented the space next door to his proctology office and opened a small drop-in center for the study of Zen. Uncle Fred says there are a lot of folks around town who'd really benefit from a good, swift, spiritual kick in the ass, and since he knows more about that most important part of the anatomy than anyone else around, he feels obliged to at least offer.

# Bronco Buster

*Erv Bobo*

Sometimes I go out to the City Art Museum and look at the casting of Remington's "Bronco Buster." Sometimes I just pick up the old rifle, the broken stock held together with baling wire and a leather splice, and I think about Dad. For a long time, all I had of him was less than a piece of wire or a splice.

My dad was the best bronco buster in the state of Illinois.

That may seem small to those who think the only wild horses were west of Kansas, but the job called for as much courage as was ever had by any Wyoming buster.

This story is not a tale about riding a horse that nobody else could ride, for Dad did that a hundred times. In fact, in those days, if you had a horse that couldn't be broken or ridden, you just naturally called on Hamer Bobo. It wasn't an occupation that paid much, but it did have a heavy cost.

Dad had to reach for courage early. When he was fourteen years old, something went wrong with his left leg. The first operation—the one to explore the mystery—was done in the farmhouse on the kitchen table. The light came from a kerosene lamp held by his father, and there was no anesthetic.

For the second operation, after a deterioration of the thighbone was found, the family sold what they could, borrowed money from relatives and got the boy down to St. Louis. When he came back, a section of the bone had been replaced by a silver rod. Since he didn't have his full growth at the time, this left him with one leg shorter than the other and kept him from marching off to World War I.

Hamer had been breaking horses before the war. With all the energy of a boy, he thrived on the excitement, and after the first time or two, he found he had a talent for the job. Those who have ridden broncs will tell you that a good part of it is gritting your teeth and hanging on. I maintain he learned how to hang on during that night on the kitchen table, but my sister disagrees. She says Dad was born as wild as the horses he rode and nothing but an act of God could ever have changed him.

When the war did come, there were more horses to be broken. Sometimes they were brought in herds from Wyoming and Colorado and when Dad was through with them they went through a chain of buyers and sellers until they wound up in France. Artillery used up horses quick, and there was always a demand for more.

They say these herds were brought in by real cowboys from out in the real west and that Dad outrode the best of them. There are still a few people around who saw it first hand, so I can't doubt their words when they say these horses were as wild as any and meaner than most that you'll find in a rodeo.

And there is this: in a rodeo, the rider only has to stay on the horse for eight seconds. Dad had to stay on or keep getting back on until the horse knew who was the boss.

It was like a rodeo when Dad had a string to break. Farm work would stop and men from all over the county would gravitate to where Dad was working; they would sit on the fences or on their farm wagons. They say he'd sit on a fence himself, studying the horse. Likely as not he'd out with a cigarette paper and a sack of Country Gentleman tobacco and have himself a smoke while he thought whatever it is riders think about.

Then he'd mount while others held the blindfolded horse, and when he had his seat he'd yell, "Let her go!" and the show was on, and those who were betting men were cheering loudest of all.

Now it needs to be said they weren't betting against Dad. They were just betting on how long it might take, how many rides before the horse was subdued enough to stand a harness or a saddle.

Rodeo riders will tell you there never was a horse couldn't be rode and never was a cowboy couldn't be throwed. Dad and his horse came together some time after the war. By then, the demand for horses had waned and except for a few amateur rodeos up and down the state, Dad mostly tended the family farm.

The hard money earned during the war years was just as hard to earn, but there was a lot less of it. Hamer Bobo was thirty-three, and that is old for a job that jars your bones and twists every muscle in your body, but a man trying to make a living at the beginning of the Great Depression couldn't turn down two dollars, no matter how hard the work.

As horses went, this one was nothing special. It wasn't black as night; no one had given it a scary name—or any name at all, for that matter. It may have been a horse no one could ride, but no one knew, for none had tried.

Dad sat on the rail and smoked while they blindfolded the horse and brought him out to the snubbing post. Then he jumped down, ground out the cigarette with a boot that had seen too many years. He mounted the horse, yelled for it to be let go and raked it with his spurs.

People who were there said they'd seen him ride tougher horses though this one was not easy by any measure. It was all over the corral, trying to brush Dad off against the rail fence, kicking higher that a tall man's hat. When none of that worked, the horse started to sunfishing, getting all four feet off the ground and curving his spine sideways, like a fish when it's pulled out of the water. The horse miscalculated on one of these jumps and man and horse came crashing down against the snubbing post.

Friends who were there said Dad was trapped but he never let go the reins or called for help. The farmer and his sons started toward the horse, who was flailing the air with his forelegs, but Dad shouted them back.

Man and horse were mostly on their left sides, with Dad's leg pinned against the post. He held onto the reins and with his right hand and right spur he began to work the horse over. Dad got a grip on the horse's ear and pulled his head around while he bloodied the flank with his spur. After what seemed like a long, long time, the horse got the idea that he could only relieve the pain by moving in that direction and slowly he got his feet on the ground and managed to stand.

Hamer Bobo held on, gritting his teeth, and when the horse got to his feet Dad was still mounted. I wish I could have heard the cheering, even though it came from only twenty or thirty men. I wish I had known him then instead of so much later, but it all happened before I was born and that was the last unbroken horse Dad ever rode.

The fall against that snubbing post left his leg raw and bleeding, but that would heal. What would never heal was the bend it put in that silver rod that was a substitute for bone. That it could have been replaced was unquestionable. Equally unquestionable was the fact that there was no money for such a thing, and in the future Dad could foresee, there never would be any.

The bend left his leg dished in at the thigh and though he could walk the limp was terrible. One thing I know about those days is that he gave away his spurs. One thing I know he kept, for it was still in the house when I was a boy, was a blank starter pistol. In his days with the rodeo, he and others would fire these out the windows of trains to hurrah the town in which they were performing. Now it is gone, and I have no idea what became of it. For a long time, I had no idea what became of that man on horseback.

I think each of us has a central time in his life, a time when what we see is diamond-sharp, what we smell is ripe and fragrant, what we hear has a clarity that will never come again. For many men of Dad's century, their time came during the wars. I like to think Dad's time came when he was young and breaking horses, but I don't know.

Nor do I know whether it is right that some of us keep those times close to the forefront of our memories. It may be that the true measure of a man is to live his central time and then to live beyond it.

They say Dad cut quite a figure in his cowboy dress and could have taken up with just about any girl in the county. Once he quit riding, he did take a wife. On the application for the marriage license, he listed his occupation as "cowboy," but that was the last thing he ever did that had to do with cowboying. And the only things he took with him from that time were the starter pistol, a terrible limp, and the courage to put it all behind him.

I suppose my mother had as much courage as my Dad, to be only fourteen years old and to try to make a marriage in the worst times of the Depression. After the ceremony before a justice of the peace, they went to the grocery store and then to a park across the street. A nickel's worth of baloney and some crackers was what they had for a wedding dinner.

Another war came, and we moved to town, close to St. Louis. It is from those times that I remember playing with the starter pistol and remember how Dad would make me breakfasts of bread and milk gravy, how he would take me with him to the corner tavern. I don't recall that he ever held my hand when we walked, but I do remember teasing and the way his eyes shut tight and his shoulders shook when he laughed.

Dad worked nights as a switchman on the railroad, and during the day my mom welded airplanes for Curtiss-Wright. There, she met city people and learned city ways. Today, I suppose we'd say she became liberated. I don't know if there was a word for it then.

It was during this time, when Mom's brothers were returning from the war, that the fighting between them began. I understood none of it, but by the time I was five they were divorced. Dad went back to the farming country while the rest of us stayed in the city. He visited a few times and always remembered to bring me a Bull Durham sack filled with hazelnuts, and then I didn't see him for thirty years.

I heard of him now and then. My brother and sister, both older, visited him over the years, but I would not. Being the youngest, I didn't know him as well as they did, and I more easily absorbed the venom that is spread around when a family dissolves. I didn't hate him; I simply had no interest in him.

When my mom's mother died, Dad came to the funeral. We said pleasant hellos but little more, but on the way home my wife said, "I like your dad."

I grunted something in reply.

"You should go see him sometime. Maybe you just need to get to know him."

I thought it would be hard to find anything to say to him after all those years, but when my wife finally wore me down, and we paid him a visit, there was little awkwardness. He was old now, too old for farming or any other kind of work, and his income was from Social Security.

During the visit, he gave my wife a .22 rifle, saying he had no more need of it. It was old, much of the bluing gone, the stock broken but held together with a nailed leather splice and baling wire. But it shoots true, truer than any rifle I've ever handled, and I will never have it repaired.

It was during this visit that he turned the talk to eating fish and after a while slapped his knee and said, "By God, let's go get some fish."

Along the Illinois River are countless stands selling fresh fish, but each time I asked about stopping he told me to drive on. Soon we came to the town of Kampsville, and he directed me to a tavern where he bought a gallon of wine. On the way back to his home, I asked again about fish and he said, "Oh, hell. Pull in anywhere."

Back at his house, my wife offered to cook for him and he said, "I don't want any damned fish. You kids take 'em home with you."

That evening, I called my brother to let him know I'd visited Dad and his first words were, "Did he pull the fish scam on you?" The scam was Dad's way of getting to a wet county where he could buy wine.

There's not a lot more to tell. My wife and I visited him now and then over the next few years, and Dad lived long enough to meet the two children we produced. By then, the crippling was bad enough that he could only move around with a walker. Alone, he spent most of his time at the kitchen table, sipping a mixture of wine and lime Kool-Aid, playing solitaire, and still rolling his own cigarettes.

There were a few paperback books in evidence, all of them western novels, and I wondered if he still thought of himself as a cowboy. I didn't ask. Someday I'll know what old men dream of, and my dreams will be as private as I allowed his to be.

It did not seem a good life, but he didn't want any more. Instead of taking help from us, he gave me what money he had—a payoff from cancer insurance—and insisted I use it to start bank accounts for my children.

One day, he talked about a time he had worked on a farm in Oklahoma. He told how the farmer and his wife had several children who looked to him for entertainment, in a day and place when strangers were about the only entertainment to be had. Because he was tired at the end of the day, the only way he could keep the kids from clambering over him was to steel himself against them, be indifferent to their pleas. He said he guessed he'd stayed that way.

I think now he may have been telling me why he never sat me on his lap, why he never ruffled my hair.

When he died and my sister and I were making the funeral arrangements with an undertaker who had lived in the county all his long life, my sister made a strange request.

"You knew Dad all his life, didn't you?" she asked the undertaker.

"I certainly did. Most of it, anyway. I'm about ten years younger than him."

"Well...I know this sounds silly, but for the last twenty years or so he's been so stooped that I can't remember how he was when I was young. Was he a tall man?"

"Miss Jackie, I'm the wrong man to ask about that." He smiled and looked beyond us, remembering down the years. "I do remember when your dad was breaking horses. And when he wasn't, he'd be walking around town in that big hat and those cowboy boots. I was there when he rode that last horse."

My sister shook her head, not understanding.

"Miss Jackie, to me your dad was always ten feet tall."

I think about that now and then. I think about a rifle and a man, both held together with spit and baling wire, both enduring the long years.

Remington's "Bronco Buster" was cast in bronze. So was mine.

# Battlefield

*Ann E. Gerike*

In early morning light washed bright by rain,
Flushed out of hiding by the pounding storm,
Fat earthworms litter black macadam roads.

Some pressed to paste,
Some move with, for an earthworm, frantic haste.
Some lie unmoving—dead?—until I nudge
Their tender length with my white Reebokked toe.

I say to my companion, Which is best?
To struggle back to safety in the earth
And move a little longer through the dark,

Or to stretch out, exposed,
Perhaps be lifted, ferried through the air
And have a crow's-eye view of all the world,
Be shredded by a beak, thrust down a throat—

Or possibly to simply rest
And dry, and die there, in the sun

# Gardening with Pen in Hand

*Eva Shaw*

Curious? I'm not suggesting you plant petunias with a ballpoint or flip the compost heap with a fountain pen. I am asking you to look at the possibilities that grow out of keeping a garden journal. It's good for the soul, it's good therapy, it's a good way to replenish and grow.

Just today I've received a new one, a hard cover that's stripped like garden onions, with a silky marigold-colored ribbon to mark the progression of my journaling. It was a surprise from Becky, a kind new friend, and I am savoring the journal and getting to know this bright woman.

The journal is pristine, clean and fresh, much like my cutting garden was less than a year ago. Soon the journal will be spilling over with words like my new garden. Gardens and journals are much the same—they start with dreams. The one in my front yard was a birthday present from my husband and son. They hauled bricks, sweated over cement, wheeled in topsoil, all in the name of love. I choose the flowers. I dug in the dirt. I worked to create a bit of paradise joining with Nature.

I planted sweet peas, for fragrance, and since their season is short, they tell me to cherish life, reminding me that we do not know the number of our days. I planted bulbs by the dozen. I loved their surprise factor. I can never remember just where I've planted them and BAM! They pop up in unexpected places. They take me to a time when as a child I was ill, feverish and miserable. Mama arranged a handful of King Alfred daffodils in a crystal vase and placed them near my bedside. It was my first grown up bouquet and formed a part of me that continues, these years later, to share her "flowers make you feel better" philosophy as I give bouquets away.

Daisies are in the garden because they're part of my history. When my husband and I were first married, barely making ends meet and living far from anywhere I could garden, he splurged one payday showering me with a small bouquet of daises. In our nearly thirty years together, I've been given far more expensive gifts, but the daisy remembrance is wrapped in the velvet of precious memories. I must ask him if he remembers...I am sure he does.

Sunflowers are in my cutting garden although I cannot get myself to cut these beauties as they tower over the garden fence and flaunt their faces to the world. They tell me it's good to be sturdy and stand out from the crowd.

A journal is like a garden where we "plant" our ideas, some perhaps too dear to share and some that are better left as secrets. We can place words on paper to write out, scratch out, rewrite and ponder at silent moments.

With this glorious new journal, I could have held back and started writing on the first day of summer. I considered beginning at the first of the month. That's what the "logical me" shouted as I found my favorite pen. But why? There are no rules to journaling as there are no right or wrong ways to garden.

In all journal writing and even on slips of paper, I write the date. I'll do so with my entries because it feels right, and besides the days blend quickly, a designation marks times in our lives. Someday when I'm older, I may want to think back and marvel at my (possibly misspent) youthful middle age. Perhaps I'll laugh and shake my head at this time when I tried to juggle dozens of writing and teaching projects, bundles of responsibilities while growing delicate Canterbury bells, hearty nasturtiums, and even delicate herbs with a garden full of marauding slugs barely waiting until twilight to pay a visit.

Taking time to write in a garden journal feels odd, especially if we're not practiced at jotting down thoughts, plans and even jumbled ideas. Knotty memories may shoot up and we may wonder if they're weeds or the sprouts of something to be cherished. Sometimes we have to wait and see.

In our garden journal we need not censor or explain. The book can be for our eyes only, to be hidden away from others. That's the "job" of a journal.

I love to make lists, from what to get at the grocery store to what to achieve in life. My goals will be found in that journal; I can feel them budding now. I will write what's in bloom and the reason I've selected it. Gardening and writing remind us that we need not be perfect. That's God work, not ours, so in my journal I will admit Black Thumb failures in ghastly detail and then move on. Guilt free.

Journaling about the garden isn't great literature. When intending to write "important" thoughts, I become pretentious, my sentences convoluted. Rather than write that the apple tree is full of blossoms and bees, bouncing like children on a sugar high, I tend to gush with words Wadsworth would choke on. I'm not a formal or prissy gardener, why write thoughts that way? I want to write about the colors, fragrances, touch and taste of my scrap of Mother Earth. My journal is a book of thanksgiving to God.

Many famous gardeners and writers, from Gertrude Jekyll to Thalassa Cruso, share memoirs in the "Year In The Garden" formats, but that's not in my plans. When the pages run out in this one, I'll start another. I want the memories to be me. I don't care if someone thinks I'm dim-witted or silly because I gush over a Double Delight rose or get gaga hugging October's bounty of scarlet leaves. I hope you'll vow the same.

If my words, ideas and this humble journal survive to some future date, so be it, but I'm not planning that now. Okay, there is a tiny part of me that hopes my garden journal will be read by grandchildren or great grandchildren. I wish my grandmothers had kept journals. So if for nothing but the future, I'll write. Someday, perhaps from this beautiful new journal, a yet unborn child will say, "I'm planting sweet peas. Great Grandmother Eva adored them." Of course, this reader will know that in 2002, only lavender sweet peas produced flowers. That "fact" will disappear unless it's in my journal.

Write from the heart and revisit thoughts and feelings. Doing so you can again be part of a June day within your words, breathing in rose geranium or nibbling on a sprig of peppermint.

I'm going to place flowers between the pages, perhaps a snapshot of my garden, maybe a bit of poetry, maybe a photograph of my Welsh terrier, Buttons. I will add garden-variety quotes that stir me and copy the URL's of websites I cannot do without.

Writing in a garden journal or for that matter any new habit, whether it's good or bad, takes about six weeks to become established. In order to make this a regular part of my life, I've designed a special time each day to write about my garden. Late afternoon appeals to me when I escape from being a wife, mom, writer and housekeeper. I am going to sit in a lawn chair, in a shady spot as the shadows string out and the birds zoom madly in my garden, determined to snap up dinner-sized worms. .

What will I write? What will YOU say? I'm a simple person and will scribble, "Today I've started this garden journal. With paper and pen I will tell myself about my garden."

It's my hope you write about the breezes on your face, the soil on your fingers and the sunshine on your back, amongst other miracles. I pray you'll take up gardening with pen in hand.

# With a Little Help from Raven

*Duane Niatum*

Our story begins so long ago that not one of the animal people in the village, alive or dead, remembers who told the story first. Mink claims that he does not mean to brag but that it was his gift to the people; Raven says Mink lies through his fur but that he would rather not say who gave it to the people. Blue jay lifts his crest and gives his raucous refrain that he heard the story from a cedar cone; the Cone told him to pass it on to the people. Cone warned that if he didn't do this, Thunderbird would eat it before the village fire turns to coal and the people's bones start the shakers' dance for the midnight hour. Thunderbird remembers it was long before humans became the destroyers of everything they looked at or touched. Old One thinks it was when the animal people gathered together to talk over what were the real problems twisting their nerves and stealing their sleep. Raven thinks it was definitely the age before the world changed, when people acted like animals and animals acted like people. In this respect Crow guesses the age was hardly different than our own, an age when people either run themselves down to bone or turn themselves into fat vats on the fast track and move in and out of nowhere and arrive at a second more lopsided nowhere in such great style that skunk and flea look almost jealous. Yet, each person in the village could see with little problem that the world was upside down, and they were seeing it from the inside out. So, who is happy and singing like a wolf in spring? The people were beginning to ask themselves this before breakfast, after lunch, and even at dinner. Furthermore, the people were not overjoyed with the way the world was spinning off its axis at that age, either. Then, there was the question of the rivers...why the rivers ran in five directions at once was one thing they hoped to talk about at the gathering. The village echoed the whole Olympic Peninsula - "Life's difficult enough without us needing to worry about where the rivers are going to turn next." The Village family was in agreement, of course, that the ducks, geese, great blues, and scoters, were distant relatives, even the oyster catcher, but the people were delighted that these family members had their own villages and ceremonies, to speak nothing of places to go and fish to tongue. There was one thing, however, that the people could agree on at this Powwow. They elected Eagle to be the headman of the feast and gathering. Eagle would let them in on the story of how to turn their square lives back to a circle and uncross their eyes and toes.

Eagle had himself a nice round-house of sticks tossed and dropped at random on the top of a very tall, black cottonwood tree near the river. The nest looked like a swamp lodge, but no wind ever wrinkled Eagle's feathers, no storm ever weakened his grip on the horizon or his taste for fish stories. Yes, those sticks were touched with magic and held the nest together like thorned love. So, when the people failed to make some decision or act on something before it was too late, they would step beneath the tree and call up to the one with the yellow-masked beak and ask what they should do to get themselves free of the indecisive snare they had created for themselves.

Yes, every person in the village believed Eagle would show them how to stop their stomachs from churning back and forth like a whirlpool. Eagle, if he was not deeply engrossed in eye-balling every step a creature made through the forest with those telescopic eyes of his, or dreaming in his cliff-gliding way of a salmon barbecue, he would call down to the people with a few choice words he had been saving up for just such an event. The people were in awe of the sunset-bird with the hair-lock, because he never once dropped his orator's staff out of the nest. The people were grateful to old fish-claws; they were told as children that his staff also served as a club, when necessary, so no one far below looking skyward from the trunk of the tree wanted to feel how old yellow-eyes' staff could indent its story on their skull.

During the events at the gathering, all animals in the village had an opportunity to tell the rest of the community what they thought were the crucial issues facing them. The people loved this democratic way of playing out their lives and taking care of business. They had not yet joined the club of conspicuous consumption nor did they yet carve in their sculptures who was at the top of the pole and who was at the bottom.

Nevertheless, the great mother-of-the-earth believed the people had been arguing day and night, rain or shine, feast or famine, summer or winter, for longer than even the ticks could endure, about which way the rivers should run. Some people thought it would be best for all concerned if the rivers flowed directly down the mountains to the sea. Others thought that was a foolish idea and that the rivers should climb quickly up the mountains. A clan from a distant village believed the rivers should flow both ways, yet they remained silent on how this was to be accomplished. Still, the majority of the people continued to demand, except Raven, that each river should flow up one side of a mountain and down the other side, like gravity pulling back the tide. They voted for each river to travel up the mountain as far as the falls, and then be good enough to turn around and flow back down to the Big-pond's edge.

Then one afternoon when the people were particularly calm and feeling their roots were well grounded and not cottonwood fluff in the air, they looked up to Eagle and asked him what he thought of their plan? Eagle heard the people call him seriously and intently, so he rolled his head from side to side and flapped his wings one quick beat before he peered down at them and answered, "It looks like you got a plan. Go for it. The rivers should run both directions so that the new people who arrive will have an easy time keeping on the trail. It will be a piece of cake for them to go upstream, and another piece of cake to return back downstream. However, maybe we should ask Raven what he thinks of the idea. Thus Eagle called to Raven, and Raven agreed to let the people in on his moon-combed tail in the wind opinion.

"I don't mean to throw a stink bug in the chowder," replied Raven, "but if the rivers turn around at the falls, how will the salmon people have a chance to stop for a breather? They will ripple their way up the mountain to the falls, and then turn their noses back downstream to the mouth of the river and open sea. So, I ask the people, with such a plan, where will the salmon people spawn? In addition, how will the new people catch them? Now, if you ask me, I think all the rivers would feel their best if they could flow in one direction, from the top of the mountains downward to exchange songs with the white-tailed waves of the sea."

Beaver beat his tail-drum on the ground three times and was the first person to say that he considered Raven to have the right idea. He reminded the people at the gathering that, "We would have a tough time surviving, if the rivers flowed both ways."

"That's it," says Raven. "Beaver sees the magic in the water dance. It just makes perfect sense to ask the river spirits to help the river flow with ease but one way. Therefore, I suggest we create a paddle song for the salmon people on their trek upstream. Furthermore, at all the bends in the streams, rivers, and creeks, there should be little eddies. The eddies will help the salmon slow down and catch their breath for the final leap into our lives. And at these eddies the people will hunt in the manner of dream catchers, currents, and wavy scales. From the depths of my shadow side, I see this the lure to good fishing."

"Raven's words are a strawberry feast," said Eagle from his lodge at the top of the cottonwood.

"Raven's story strikes us as sound as a log drum," the people of red cedar all agreed. In fact, in about the space of time it takes a mosquito to bite her way into our story, their faces were beacons of delight, and they chanted the magic song of agreement until dawn and the first glimpse of the morning star—"Caw! Caw! Caw!" Thus, from that time of gathering the people have followed a similar destiny to this day. Our grandfather still tells the children during our winter storytelling ceremony, for this simple reason, all the rivers run but one way. He shows us this is beauty's trail through the mountains and forests, and this is why the salmon leap and snap their tails and pound every cell in their bodies up the home river each year to spawn in the gravel beds. And with the final notes of the sunset song, in the steady light of Evening star, the salmon can let go of their quest, the long and difficult journey from the depths and distances below and through the corridors that are so dark the sea, too, is a blind mother and swept away.

Afterword: The inspiration for writing this adaptation of a Klallam sacred narrative is to lend support to all the Klallams at Lower Elwha, Jamestown, and Port Gamble who are encouraging the young people to learn the language, songs, and stories of their ancestors. I hope the modern context for the story will help draw them into its world. Furthermore, key figures in the narrative are also youths, and this too, should appeal to their interest. We have passed the point where we can ignore the fact that the Klallam language is endangered, and with it our oral traditions. For decades even before I was born, the forces of Euroamerican culture, particularly those of the missionaries, federal government and educators, succeeded in convincing or shaming American Indian children and youth into ignoring or resisting all connections to their tribal heritage. The Language Preservation Center at Lower Elwha was created several years ago to turn that around.

# Fin de Siècle
## Sonnet Out of Town

*Richard Robbins*

*—western Utah*

Across the salt flat, white-hot and miles wide,
hills cut the surface like black fins. Roads end there
if you believe your eyes. Gulls trade in their
first and only question, hovering, for that high
circle of mockery, what birds must have cried,
until Mormons came to stay, when sickened herds
gave out, when ox carts overturned
and the westward passage died, all those eyes

left here for pecking. Meanwhile, the wavy
highway, black as a stalled car or hill,
disappears in basalt. Where would the century
have me go? Not back. Not west. Nowhere still
ground zero, the earth all glass. Nowhere leaves
don't shade the grosbeak, don't wrinkle on the sill.

# Laying Down One's Life

*Christin Chaya*

Sitting next to my dad, a cherished event, jostling along in the big yellow stock truck...we are making our way on dirt roads running the fence lines between ranches. Stopping on each side of the gates is a precise ritual I have come to know as I have learned the importance of being tuned in to its delicate timing.

As we drive, my eyes behold the dance of the shifting-pattern as I straddle the gears. I watch my dad's hand move, in perfect synchrony with the clutch, and I know just when I need to move my left leg more into his. My life seems punctuated by these moments.

Today there is no fear, just my good fortune that I can come along for this monthly chore. I do not care what it is, I just love being with my dad. Both older and younger brothers are there as well, but, unlike me, they do not attach any deeper meaning or feeling to what might be shared beneath the outer chore.

The truck rattles into the barnyard, pulling up to and almost touching the chutes; Dad checks the mirrors as the rushing sound of the air brakes signals the completion of our arrival. We climb out; the men open the door to the chutes and unload the stock. Just two steers...looking up at us as we go about our business walking back and forth on the running boards.

My dad reaches into the truck for his revolver. His eyes become soft as they so often do, and I know he is saying a prayer. He has told me about this, that there is no greater gift than to lay down one's life for a friend. I stand very close to him as he gently marks the first steer....mapping out diagonal lines between eyes and ears. Where the lines invisibly intersect, he shoots the bullet. The piercing sound coincides with the steer dropping to the ground, ending that moment of terrible silence just before. And then everyone is busy.

The bottom panel of that chute opens out onto the slaughterhouse floor, water running across the cold concrete. We walk around to the door and cross the room. I jump up to my designated seat on top of the storage freezer, out of the way, and watch as my dad and brothers butcher the steer. The sharp knife slits neck and throat. Gushing blood swirls with the water down the drain. They tip up the hindquarters to pour all the blood out, hoist the rear legs, and slit an opening through the middle. In what seems like only minutes, they have transformed a living being into a carcassobject. They follow a routine, and by the time the men are just working on sides of beef, they are back to their usual banter and laughter. We are having a good time, and I am grateful to be included.

One down and one to go. We go back out to the chutes, the day is brilliant and warm...refreshing after the slaughterhouse flesh and blood smell. The second steer is run into the chute. Once again, my dad reaches into the truck for his revolver. His eyes become soft as they so often do, and I know he is saying a prayer. I stand very close to him as he gently marks this steer....mapping out diagonal lines between eyes and ears. I look down into those eyes. I am startled by how they are looking at me. I hasten to remind myself about the service his life is giving. I try to make it all right. The moment seems to hang there, everything frozen, and then the shot rings out like some terrible scream into the bright summer day. But the steer is still standing, bawling loudly with his head raised up over the sideboards, his eyes rolling— catching mine again.

Dad runs to the truck to reload, and runs back to fire again into a point just behind the ear. The steer bawls, shakes his head and looks at us. More shots, and my dad is swearing. Frantic movement and sounds blur and stagger like nightmare film images unhinged. I am afraid of this steer that refuses to die, but also am afraid that Dad is angry at me. The steer drops to his knees, emitting a chilling sound. Dad shouts to my brothers, "Jason, let him drop through. Peter, slit his throat."

I follow my brother into the slaughterhouse and jump up onto the freezer. He has the knife, slicing through hide and throat of this steer still partially propped on its knees. Blood gushes out onto the floor, but the steer manages to get up onto all fours again, charging towards my brother. My brother runs out, slamming the door behind him, yelling for my dad. I sit, unmoving, my gaze locked with the steer's....as he stands there, swaying...blood pouring onto the floor...his head almost disconnected, yet a sound comes from his throat.

The door bursts open—more shots, more shouts, more anger. The steer finally goes down, and everyone works furiously...no talking now. The chore is completed, the carcass is skinned and hanging, just another side of beef. However, my dad says he will mark this one, and that we will not eat of it.

On the way home, at the first gate my dad tells me that I will not be allowed to accompany him when butchering anymore. There are some other words, but I cannot understand them, I cannot take them in. I am lost in my own swirl of water and cold and blood inside, through the searing pain of being told I cannot be with him. He says something about my not letting the steer die, and I want to cry. I silently plead with both God and my dad, "Please don't make it be my fault. "

At the final gate, through silent tears, my eyes behold the dance of the shifting-pattern as I straddle the gears. I watch my dad's hand move, in perfect synchrony with the clutch, and I know just when I need to move my left leg more into his. It is a solemn and silent return home. He must not know that he is breaking my heart.

We never spoke of it.

# Goya's Monsters

*Norton Girault*

When they exhumed your skeleton in 1888,
Sixty years after your decease,
To send it back to Spain from France,
The skull was gone (purloined and never found again.)
Madrid wired the Spanish consul at Bordeaux:
DISPATCH GOYA WITH OR WITHOUT HEAD.

"The sleep of reason produces monsters,"
You wrote beneath Caprice No. 43, in which,
Around the shoulders of a sleeping man, slumped face
down on desk,
Demon bats and owls befoul the air—
This the mildest
Of your monster dreams.

And the Black Paintings—
Wild-eyed, naked Saturn
Biting off the arms and head
Of his unswaddled son.
You are one of many who have tried
To exorcise the violence of the world.
Saturn, devouring his children
Was not your idea.
The Greeks blamed that on their celestial father-figure.
You simply made it flesh, as did Reubens that you studied,
No less horrific.

Was Reason in control when you painted those passionate

portraits
Of patrons, wife, children, yourself?
And the nude Maja, your Duchess of Alba of the burning
eyes?
Was Reason your defense against monsters
When you admired the French Revolution,
Before The Disasters of War and the Black Paintings?
The nobility of your bulls,
Even in their onslaughts on spectators and their goring of
matadors,
Did Reason say that ritual made that right?

When the French came, you were no patriot,
Did not fight in the streets as even Spanish women did
With kitchen knives and scythes and flails,
You painted: Always the sufferings of civilians.
Severed heads, limbs dangling from trees.
In "Madrid, 3rd May, 1808:
Executions at the Mountains of Prince Pius,"
The central figure of those condemned
Flings his arms crucifixion-wide at the firing squad,
His disbelieving eyes seeming to cry out
To Napoleon's aiming soldiers:
"I believed in your revolution! I believed in Reason!"

Who robbed that tomb in Rue Coupe-Gorge in 1888?
Some mad phrenologist searching for the demon lump?

# Down at The Igloo

*Brian Ames*

Down at The Igloo a cut-up man walked in one evening. The summer sun was dropping in the west down Evergreen Boulevard past a service station and the memorial park. The sun threw its rays sideways onto him, the slices in his T-shirt, the cuts, blood welling and coagulated in spots. That T-shirt seemed to glow orange from within, and he dragged a long shadow as he entered. The cut-up man looked as if he had encountered an unhappy cloud of wildly kinetic blades, lacerated from the crown of his head to his midriff.

From The Igloo's nest of chrome and Formica, from behind the counter, I stared at the cut-up man. Alice the fry-cook sat on a stool behind me, overhovering the idle grill, gaze buried in the furrow of a spine-bent paperback. The cut-up man was the first human being we'd encountered in more than an hour. The grill was hot. Alice had shaped roundels of raw burger into patties. She'd primed the heat on the twin wells of french-fry oil. But she had yet, at that point, to actually cook anything. And by now, she had abandoned to her paperback story any idea that she soon would. After giving me a directive or two, she was otherwise engaged. She didn't notice the little goat bell that rang when the door opened, the cut-up man's entry.

I had been listening to the radio, staring out the drive-through window, which was opposite the door for walk-ups. Suddenly a beetle dropped itself onto the drive-up shelf, inverted, so that its carapace and wings lay on the Formica. Its thorax pointed up, six legs beating air like rotors. I had watched the bug for a while—it was pretty, iridescent I'd say, thinking back today, fat and unique. I'd never seen an insect of its type around where we lived. It struggled to right itself for a few minutes, then I slid open the side window, flicked it out into the parking lot with my index finger. It bounced on the asphalt, all clacking exoskeleton, and flew off just as I heard the goat bell.

The cut-up man was short and gaunt. I, at seventeen, was already taller and more muscular. I would have placed him in age somewhere around forty or forty-five—it was difficult to tell by his wounded face and structure. Because he entered and immediately stood still, I couldn't observe how he carried himself, what about him a gait would reveal. If you discounted the fresh blood, his T-shirt was fairly clean, no doubt a men's small, the sleeves high up on the biceps. It was neatly cut in places, and I could see the red canyons of shallow wounds underneath. He wore a pair of jeans that had faded to near white on the front of the thighs. There was a bloodstain or two on them as well.

As the cut-up man turned to look at me full on, I noticed that the area around his mouth was swollen and bright red, pre-bruised if that makes any sense. A little runlet of blood had welled over the corner of his lips, dropped from his chin. The hair on my arms disappeared into gooseflesh mounds, the center of my stomach clenched. I felt my digestive tract flop and wind on itself. What had happened here? Could whatever violence had broached this man's world have followed him into The Igloo? Was I, was Alice, at risk? I didn't know how to begin a conversation with a cut-up, mouth-bashed man. I wondered about the rules of engagement.

So I asked him if I could take his order.

He didn't answer immediately, seemed to reflect on my query, start to answer, then pause. Finally, he mumbled a thick, glottal request:

"I wouldn't mind an ice-cream cone," he said.

A single wave of relief washed through me. I could do that. I could draw the cut-up man an ice-cream from the vanilla machine—I understood everything about the procedure, how to do it properly, how to hold the edible cone and swirl the soft mix into a pleasing cold shape. I looked behind me at Alice, still unaware of the cut-up man's presence. "I can get that for you," I said, turning around again. Our eyes met for just a second. In his I saw something I didn't—couldn't—recognize.

I drew a cone from its cardboard cylinder, from inside plastic wrap. I pulled the vanilla machine's lever downward with my right hand, held the cone underneath the spigot in my left and moved it in a tight circle. I appreciated the opportunity to be occupied, to not look up at the man. I finished it perfectly, the whir of the machine's manifolds accompanying the last twisting flourish at the top of the cone. A tiny loop of the cream bent back on itself in a frosty perfect arc.

I hesitated offering the cone across the counter, wondering whether his hand would touch mine, whether those fingers—which, yes, had abrasions and blood, too—would graze mine. The cut-up man accepted the ice cream, seemed to examine it for the best approach, a route across it. He lifted it toward his battered lips, obliterated the loop and its swirling root in icy, sucked contact. As he drew his hand away, the brightest red I had ever seen blotted the pearly ice cream. The blood reminded me of a drop of oil in water—it seemed to spread and glow.

He licked at the cone twice more, oblivious to the blood. It must have cooled his fractured lips, a tongue that was undoubtedly cut or bitten. I noticed one of the cuts on his forearm freshly well and ooze, then a subsequent splash of blood on The Igloo's spotless linoleum. It looked like a bullet wound in the tile floor. He reached for his back pocket to pay.

"You don't have to pay." I held my hands up in a gesture of negation. It was all I could think of, to offer this aching person a free ice cream. "It's all right."

He appraised my upheld hands with a weird look, moved his eyes up them to my face. I could see he understood my meaning but didn't know how to react to the kindness. He sought reaffirmation: "I don't have to pay?"

"No."

He licked the cone again then mumbled his thanks. Then he returned his attentions to the cone, looking straight at the object as he ate, not looking up or around. More blood dripped off of him. The floor was now dappled here and there under where he stood, and while some of the cuts were coagulating and some of the shirt-stains drying toward maroon, others seemed to seep more freely. Alice must have looked up from her perch and seen him for the first time just about then.

"Do you want me to call somebody?" I asked.

He looked up from the cone as if he didn't understand the question.

"A cop maybe, can I call a cop for you?" I was thinking of the patrol car that usually came around each night, up to the drive-up, for coffee. They were about an hour and a half off yet. But it's what came to mind. "You look like you've had trouble."

He nodded in agreement, although whether he agreed that he'd had trouble or that I should call a policeman for him, I'll never know.

I reached for the telephone behind the counter. I was going to call 911 and have them send an officer over. But as I poked the first digit with my fingertip, Alice's hand gently grasped my wrist and took the handset from my other hand. She placed the phone in its cradle, stood there with fleshy white arms hanging from a work blouse and unblemished apron.

She turned to the cut-up man, behind her eyes a zealous intelligence.

"You need to move on," she told him. It was a bald, raw, flat command.

He winced slightly, almost imperceptibly, with the news. He forgot about the ice cream, looked at me, then Alice. His stare now took on the look of a fellow who believed he would be struck, or stabbed, again. Still he hesitated.

"I mean it," Alice said, her voice rising a notch. "You need to be on your way."

The cut-up man turned and left. The goat bell jangled as

he opened the door, and the sounds of autos passing on Evergreen Boulevard whooshed into the still air of The Igloo. The door closed behind him, and I saw a bloodstain on the inside knob.

"Get a couple of rags," Alice said. "Clean this up."

Although she was a fry cook, I understood then that Alice knew he had his business; we had ours. There was no productive reason for his and ours to meet. I looked from her to the back of the cut-up man, outside now, walking away. He faded with the bent sunlight, walking off with his private trouble and what remained of the free ice-cream cone.

I got to work on the blood.

# Lost Puzzle Piece

*Ron Hughes*

*(For Russell)*

As if cupping his hand in mine,
I hold this piece of my son's
dinosaur puzzle that I found
in my shoe as I packed to leave.

I meant to give it to him
before I left. Now far away,
I can't return this
piece of our shared play.

Alone, it's a little bit
of cardboard splashed with color.
In the fragmented picture
it's a dinosaur's lethal claw.

With wide-eyed anticipation,
he assembles the puzzle—
each piece slapped down faster—
only to get to that dark space,

a tar pit of black emptiness,
at his beloved dinosaur's feet
that swallows the hapless animal
as it consumes my son and me.

The blackness sticks to our skin
fills our mouths, and joins us—
this incomplete father
with his unfinished son.

# In Love With Bobby

*Sharon Goldner*

Lisa Lafferman is in love with Bobby Isenberg.

No, she's never been hit over the head with a shovel, but this love thing might be as close as she gets. Lisa's head is in the heavens, and she is seeing so many stars, she could open up her head as a planetarium.

To be in the fifth grade is pretty complicated, but to throw love into the mix...well, Lisa might as well be on one of her mother's soap operas, she is so tangled up inside. Mrs. Lafferman watches all of them, you know, but she can't give her daughter any advice. All Lisa gets is "shh...wait until a commercial," but then Mrs. Lafferman goes and pees real fast, sometimes wiping herself as she is running out so as not to miss a thing. On the next commercial, she washes her hands.

Lisa's older brother, Lenny, has a chemistry set. Lisa thinks maybe he can explain the feelings she gets when she looks at Bobby Isenberg or thinks about him or even dreams of him. Her brother has diarrhea a lot. He's not supposed to eat cheese. He is never available.

Lisa Lafferman is really on her own with this Bobby Isenberg thing.

Ask Lisa, and she'll tell you that she wishes she could say that it's Bobby's intelligence (he's very good in math...Lisa ought to know; she once cheated off him on a math test), Bobby's compassion (he once kicked Lisa in the face by accident when she bent down to retrieve a pencil she dropped on purpose under his chair so she could be nearer to him to see what he smelled like. Bobby told her to "watch it," but he said it nicely. And Lisa discovered that he smelled like chocolate brownies, still hot, but cooling in a pan), or his humanity (he never made fun of her when her mother made her wear a dress to school for picture day while all the other girls got to wear their bellbottoms). But unfortunately, Lisa Lafferman has not viewed any of these character-building blocks. For her, Bobby Isenberg is just so damn beautiful.

He's got a twinkle on his face that starts in his eye and just jumps all over, crashing into his cheek and chin dimples, making the most beautiful facial collision ever. He wears these leather vest and pants outfits. He's got ten in all. He loves Elvis Presley who scares Lisa because her mother only lets her listen to The Partridge Family. She has all of their albums, don't you know. And Bobby Isenberg's got the best handwriting of anyone in the class...it's so neat and curly, like he's practiced a while, only he hasn't...it just comes out that way. Lisa thinks she should let Bobby Isenberg write all of the thank-you notes for their wedding gifts one day.

Bobby Isenberg's best friend is Garry Frankle. Lisa doesn't like him. Garry is so much like a boy...blue jeans and tee shirts, and he's always got a cut over his eye, a scrape on his knee, or a bump on his chin. He's got this thick curly hair that Lisa thinks is like a hair galaxy spinning out of control.

Garry Frankle speaks to Lisa one time. "Look at my long sideburns," is what he says on that occasion. The class is doing fractions at the time and Lisa doesn't get real numbers, let alone two on top of each other, separated by a math stick, so she doesn't look at his sideburns that are long.

He never speaks to Lisa again.

Instead, he knocks her arm, always the one with the pen at the end of it so she makes a long uneven scribble somewhere down the page...the teacher is always remarking, "what's this?" Lisa knows the teacher is writing it up on her permanent records.

It works like this: Garry Frankle sits next to Lisa on her right side. He has her deliver notes to his girlfriend, Jane Levine, who sits next to Lisa, separated by an aisle. Lisa never does this for Garry Frankle, an icky boy who farts after lunch and says, "It wasn't me." Then he does it again, sometimes not so easily so his face will bunch up a little bit red and you'd swear the curls on his head's top are going to pop right off, hitting someone in the eye. After his second emission, he goes, "Hey, that wasn't me either," and all the boys laugh and laugh, and Jane stands so proud like he'd just farted the Mona Lisa.

Lisa passes the notes for Jane. She is reading "Love Story," and Lisa thinks that's incredible, the way Jane carries it on top of her loose-leaf, her hands slung over the book so you can read the title. Mrs. Lafferman keeps her copy up high, and she does a mean fingerprint scan on the polished furniture, so Lisa doesn't even dare.

Lisa thinks if she does this note passing thing, Jane will allow her into the inner circle of popular girls, and fun girls, and girls that boys like, and they will give Lisa a wonderful boyfriend, and she can scrawl his name into the denim of her loose-leaf, in a heart with arrows and stars. Lisa thinks a boyfriend will let her wear his ID bracelet, so big and heavy that it weighs Lisa down, lopsiding her shoulder so that every year at the check-up, the doctor will have to measure how unbalanced she has become. Lisa thinks she can become friends with Jane Levine...whispering and giggling and having sleep-overs, and fun...

"You better not be reading Garry's notes to me," is how Jane approaches their non-friendship. Lisa and Jane are best non-friends to this day.

Lisa very quickly gives up on the notion of doing this for Jane Levine, for as soon as she discovers her love for Bobby Isenberg, she begins to do it for him. You see, Jane Levine used to be Bobby Isenberg's girlfriend before they broke up and she started going with Garry Frankle. Lisa doesn't want Jane to have any qualms about it. She doesn't want Jane to have any doubts, problems, second thoughts. Lisa wants Bobby Isenberg to be free, to want her. But first, she has to become alive to him. Lisa doesn't even think he knows that she breathes.

Other than the note passing, Lisa Lafferman has no idea how to get Bobby Isenberg.

The school librarian has no books on it. She says no school library carries awful books like that on love and crushes, and are they for Lisa? So Lisa fibs under the library lady's million framed pictures of Dewey who created his own decimal system—what a great man he was and how he is such a personal hero of hers. The school librarian smiles teeth like baby grand piano keys.

Lisa's best friend, Maxine Rosenblatt, is sick of the whole (Lisa wishes it was but it's not) sordid thing. Peanut butter and jelly cake Maxine's braces from lunch while she yaks about the caste system in India and how they believe you are who you are until you die.

"Are you listening to me?" Maxine screams. "It's the same thing here at school...if you're not popular to start, you're not going to be popular now. You weren't born into that group. You have to wait until you die, or at least go off to college. Even if Bobby Isenberg wanted to be with you, he couldn't. You're not in THE group."

Even more now, Lisa believes, she is really on her own here.

It doesn't help that her love for Bobby Isenberg grows, nerve endings in her brain being whittled away until what's inside her head is shaped into the outline of his name. Bobby on the brain.

On days when he's absent; on days when he gets pulled for band practice; on days when he's gone for student council meetings...Lisa's newly shaped brain swells and screams.

And then, something so unexpected happens...

Maxine Rosenblatt defies her own theories about caste.

It's another day's recess. After lunch. Outside. Lisa and Maxine are on the top bleacher in the empty softball field, practicing their yo-yo moves. It's become quite the rage at school, and the girls have finally gotten it so they aren't banging each other in the face with wayward yo-yos. They can see everybody from here...couples coupling...teachers paper-grading...athletes playing...and the unpopular kids shuffling along, damned if they'd find one another and hook up. Lisa always says the unpopulars would make the strongest and loudest group of all.

On this day, Jane Levine has to stay inside and help clean the cafeteria. She has made fun of the lunch ladies for too long a time now, and they've raised their spatulas about it.

And Garry Frankle is lost.

Lisa and Maxine watch him meander and wander, pretending to hit a homerun; pretending to karate down a bad guy; and just plain standing there sad in his jeans, melancholy spilling out of their uneven cuffs. Even his curls seem to sink down his scalp.

Maxine and Lisa smile, becoming clowns in their very own circus. And then, Maxine remarks, "If he's so lost, maybe he should fart...that ought to bring him back to himself."

Now, if Maxine would have said this at the year's beginning, Lisa would have had to ask WHAT some ten thousand times; however, Maxine's been taking drama lessons with Mrs. Farb. Maxine knows how to talk really loudly now. It's called "projecting" in the theater. Anywhere else it's called: Maxine's got a really big mouth.

Garry Frankle's ears hear Maxine's mouth. And those little auditory outlets are plenty seethed.

He jacks himself up the bleachers in no time, which is far less time than would be needed by two girls to escape. He asks for their names. Anger displaces Lisa's bones, setting up a new spine. She delivers notes for this guy all school day long and he's asking for her name...not even a health plan, not even a dental plan, not even a thank you...Lisa gets nothing from him, and now he is going to disrespect her?

"Wait a minute," he says. Even his eyebrows look like spaghetti rings. "I know you. You pass my notes. Jane says you need to pass them a little nicer. Sometimes you throw."

And then he turns to Maxine and says, "I've always felt that farting was an ancient art form that hasn't gotten its due. You're working with lethal gasses. You're working with timing. You're working with nature. Why if I didn't need it, I'd donate my ass to a museum. And now for the pleasure of you ladies, symphony in hot lunch."

He flips his rear out. The girls have never been this up close. They've never received a dedication before. Lisa and Maxine look at one another, their glasses magnifying their eyes to levels that would intimidate a microscope-secure scientist. There is no escape possible. He moves with their every attempt to get away, blowing gas from cafeteria food the experts say is nutritious, but the girls aren't sure.

Maxine mouths something. It looks like TRUST ME but she is holding her nose and breathing through her mouth so it could be anything.

"We are not amused," she projects, while he is blowing Row Row Row Your Boat, "by you. Don't you listen in Current Events? There is a gas shortage you know."

And then, Maxine defies Garry's gravity, pushing him off the bleacher, merrily, merrily, merrily, merrily, life is but a dream.

Maxine gets detention for a month. She makes friends with some of the jock girls who are in for starting a food fight. They are impressed with her pushing arm. And Maxine moves up in the caste.

Lisa gets a stern talking to about hanging out with the wrong people and being able to possess the ability to forecast the wrong-doings of others. Yeah, right, like if she could do that she would be co-hosting the Mike Douglas Show instead of being in trouble in school.

And Garry Frankle breaks his leg. His natural gas ability is diminished, but he sports a handsome cast from toe to thigh. He is also told that when the cast is off, his behavior is not to resume. "If you must," the vice principal says, "keep your...gas passing...as an extra curricular activity, outside of school, unless of course there is a medical necessity in which case you will be required to get a doctor's note. In any event, we will be watching...and smelling you." Vice principals...smaller offices and crappier jobs.

Because Lisa was up there on the bleachers unable to predict the total outcome, it is her responsibility to walk Garry ten minutes before the bell rings for the general population. Lisa is to help him get a head start to lunch, library, art, music, and everywhere really because he needs someone to carry his books, lunch, and stuff.

During these walks, he never says a word...huffing and puffing instead like some mixed-up fairytale wolf who is trying to blow these crutches down. He's clearly angry, hurt, embarrassed ...Garry won all-sports day last year, his chest decorated like a girl breaking out of training bras in a really big way. And now this. No doubt his rear end is feeling the poignancy of it all.

Jane Levine finishes reading LOVE STORY, and then breaks up with Garry...something about wanting to hang out more with her girlfriends. Personally, Lisa thinks Jane's seeking her own love story, and when Garry was out at the hospital for a week, she found a new chapter with Bruce Penn instead.

So Lisa and Garry Frankle walk the halls, quiet except for the tapping of his crutches on the speckled school linoleum. It's like they're two kids on a Saturday morning kid show, in a haunted house and the lockers are lined up like metal coffins and they never know which educational mummy is going to fall out first...a ruler, a school box, a yellow pencil that's not a number two...

And one day, Lisa tells Garry that she likes his long sideburns, and another day he asks to see what Lisa looks like without her glasses. He says, "not bad."

Days later Lisa tells him how she's loved Bobby Isenberg and he says all the girls do and he can't understand it...Bobby's just a regular guy.

A few weeks later Garry asks if Lisa loves Elvis, and at first she lies, but then she says "I don't know. I like David Cassidy, but not Bobby Sherman and not Donny Osmond," so he will think her choice is a discriminating one.

Garry Frankle asks if Lisa Lafferman knows any of the songs, and of course she does, she knows them all, and he's got sisters so he knows them too, and they both start singing I THINK I LOVE YOU over and over again some ten thousand times all the way down to the cafeteria...I THINK I LOVE YOU to nobody at all.

# What the Blind Girl Saw

*Douglas Knox*

The eight or so girls in the Brownie troop, the third that day, crowded up to my geology booth in the Youth Discovery Building at the Ohio State Fair. They looked smart in their little uniforms—brown shorts, light blue blouses, and the brown vests on which they displayed their half-dollar sized achievement patches. Each of the girls sported at least a dozen badges. This was an active troop.

My wife and I were two of the hundred volunteers working at sixteen stations for the Hands-On Science Day for Girl Scouts, our daughter's Gold Award project. The volunteers led the girls in simple experiments and discussed career opportunities with those who might be interested in a particular field. Mostly, though, we wanted to show them that science is fun. For me it was also an opportunity to share my hobby in invertebrate paleontology, the study of fossil sea animals.

The girls were as eager as trick-or-treaters on Beggars' Night, but I knew not to give myself too much credit. They weren't as concerned about what I had to tell them as the stickers I would put on their cards when I was done. Each sticker represented an activity for a badge link. The more they secured, the closer they were to earning badges. The way they shoved their cards in my face let me know that quantity was uppermost in their minds.

A movement in the background caught my eye. Glancing up from the girls, I noticed that the leader, smiling over the bedlam from behind, carried a white cane as tall as any of the girls. I took a moment to ponder the dedication she must have had to overcome less than normal vision and still direct a troop.

The girls clamored for my attention. I knew I couldn't present any technical material to them. Career tracks, rock classifications or an occasional fossil's genus-species name would have to wait for the older girls. I directed them from the display cases to the Hands-On section of the table.

They jumped to the rocks I had set out for them. By this time I knew they would skip the granites and marble, and even the higher quality fossils. Almost without exception they dove for a plain brown flat piece of sandstone about the size of a softball that contained about fifty brachiopods. It was the number of fossils in this single piece of rock that excited them.

For Brownies whose school careers hadn't progressed beyond the third grade, the fossils were simply seashells. I fielded their frenetic questions with one-sentence answers. "Yes," I told one, "they were actually little animals that lived in the water." To another, "Their shells became fossilized when they were buried under thousands of tons of sand and mud." And again, "Very good. That big one on the bottom is a shell, too."

Then one of the girls called out to the others that the next table had gumdrops. My audience dropped to about half a dozen. It was then that I noticed the girl with the sunglasses. Just little plastic, discount store glasses, nothing that stood out. Her inquisitiveness didn't express itself in quick questions. Instead she traced her fingers over the rocks, studying them with the patience of a sculptor considering her medium. The girl, not the troop leader, was sight impaired.

A few more girls left. The quiet girl stayed and found the rock with a single brachiopod, a textbook *Syringothyrus texta*. She scanned the surface of the mudstone with practiced fingertips, found the fossil, and explored it in detail. First she outlined the winged perimeter with her index finger. Then she slid her fingers over the surface, feeling the ridges and the rounded sinus.

I looked at the tilt of her head. It bore no relationship to her hands.

She wasn't sight impaired; she was blind.

The other Scouts moved on, leaving her alone with the person I now assumed to be her mother. Oblivious to the fact that her friends had deserted her, the girl groped around the table to find a place to set the rock down, and then picked up another piece of sandstone. I waited for her to find the relevant area. "This is a worm trail," I told her as she ran her fingers over the meandering, pencil-wide grove that traversed the width of the rock. "The worm slithered through the mud and made a trail just like you do when you slide your feet through the snow." She followed the trail from one side of the rock to the other.

One by one she explored the *Dictioclostus*, the *Marginifera*, and all the other brachiopods. She managed to find every fossil in the display, and I explained each one to her, fascinated at the amount of information she gleaned from them. She memorized them with her fingers.

She was careful to set each one back where she'd found it, leaving nothing disturbed. She exhibited determination that her peers would not gain until high school or even college. I was overcome with wonder at the way she approached her task. In compensating for the loss of a vital sensory apparatus, she had gained a level of maturity many times her age.

As the girl examined the rocks I tried to compose in my mind what I would say. I imagined a few unhurried moments with her mother during which I would pronounce a fitting tribute to her daughter's perception. The words would be perfect, an eloquent conclusion to a most memorable occurrence. She would know that I would never let the moment slip into obscurity.

Then without a word the girl left for the next station, her mother hurrying behind her. The abrupt end to the encounter jolted me back to reality. Instead of the anticipated conversation, I had only a single chance speak. I opened my mouth and blurted, "She's remarkable."

Where was the eloquence in that? The two-word appraisal splattered on the floor, leaving me wishing I could hide under the table.

The woman was kind to my awkwardness, however. With the barest hint of a smile and an answer that matched my commentary word for word, she called over her shoulder, "She is."

# Fog

*Kelli Russell Agodon*

      settles like sheets of insulation slipping
             from between wooden boards.
The sky, tired of living above us
        drifts down, puts its fingers in the ocean,
            lingers with waves and tugboats.

An entire island has been covered.
        We have thrown a sheet over the sofa
            to keep the dust from settling
in the homes of the dead.

Each morning, the ferry sounds
        searching haze for small boats,
            for fisherman dreaming of mermaids
they left back onshore.

# Getting the Message

*Elizabeth Engstrom*

In this world of mass marketing—from the Tostitos Fiesta Bowl, to Oprah's Book Club, to Coca Cola sponsoring the Olympic torch—it seems that the only way to reach out is by screaming. One needs a web page with flashing ads or bulletin boards that befoul the scenery or a cell phone that plays "Hail to the Chief." Everybody wants a piece of our time and attention. For a message to get across, it must be done with *presence*. And loud, apparently, is good.

But in my mind, all this fighting for our attention makes us edgy, short tempered, and prone to conflict in our own lives. Where in all this hierarchy of information-overload is the quiet moment?

It is said that conflict is the touchstone to growth. I disagree. There is no growth in conflict, except in self-recriminating retrospect. And that doesn't necessarily lead to growth. Rather, I think that most often results in retrogression and resentment.

Personally, I have never seen good come directly out of conflict. Any residual good comes as a result of our propensity as a species to seek the higher ground, to find the silver lining, to ascertain the blessing in the curse. To rise above. To be the better, bigger, higher, calmer adult.

"If there is any good to have come out of the 9/11 horror," I have heard as countless talking heads pick apart every detail ad nauseam, "it is that it has rekindled patriotism and brought our country together."

Did the terrorists get our attention? Without question. Was their message heard? Not really. Did their actions rekindle patriotism? Those who are patriots have always been. They just hadn't flown their flags lately. Did the disaster bring our country together? It is still divided over abortion, capital punishment, affirmative action and handguns. There are still murders, rapes, robberies, differences of opinion, Republicans and Democrats—not all that much has changed. We're a little more afraid on airplanes. We're a little more suspicious of our brothers and sisters of Mideastern ancestry. Is fear and suspicion a sign of growth? I think not.

When I conflict with my husband, we get nowhere. Passions escalate, tongues sharpen, forgotten wounds freshen, and if we end the discussion with a kiss, it's usually later, after one or the other of us has walked away before something damaging was said. When I conflict with the sales clerk, or the flight attendant, or the telephone company, I am not contributing to world peace. I am not promoting a life of love, mercy and ministry, those things that I endeavor to make the cornerstones of my daily activities. Who is to grow from a conflict with the IRS? Me? Or the IRS? And what does it say about us when we gleefully relate stories of conflict, especially when we announce our victory? Over what are we victorious? Certainly not our contentious animal natures.

My tiny voice has little to say in the matters of running a country, or negotiating international peace, but it is loud and strong in my personal area of responsibility.

To refuse conflict is to live a life of greater challenge and unlimited opportunity for growth. To refuse to engage in any conflict is to reason our way around it. To do that, we must have a far-reaching perspective of our place in this world. We walk through life casting seeds in our wake; are they seeds of hope, promise, spiritual riches? Or are they the seeds of doubt, distress, hate and anger? Consider that each of us is in great measure the product of the seeds we've gathered while on our path. One teacher's praise, one childhood friend's compliment, one parent's delight can mean so much. So can one insult, one racial slur, one degrading comparison. The seeds we sow spread horizontally through space and vertically through time, from coast to coast, across oceans and continents, from generation to generation.

Every day we have a handful of seeds to sow, and we drop a few every time we interact with another human being. Every time we talk with a teenager, an elderly parent, a government employee, a gas station attendant, *a telemarketer,* we're sowing seeds. If we were more conscious about fertilizing those seeds with our attitude as they're dropped onto the rich soil of another's soul, perhaps we would have more success circumventing conflict. Perhaps we would see our way around, over, under or through conflict without engaging in it. Conflict is easy; living the conflict-free life is very difficult. And a rich life is one in which we deal effectively with difficulties. Not with passive conflict avoidance, but with dynamic, life-affirming enthusiasm.

Living conflict-free is the touchstone to growth, because in the process of finding paths around the conflict, we learn that all conflict is of our own making; it's a product of our attitude. As individuals, sometimes we have control over external things and sometimes we don't, but we always have control over our attitude.

Perhaps Eugene, Oregon, where I live, with its mystique of tie-dyed flower child mixed with superb higher education, could be the center of such a philosophy. "Welcome to Eugene," the sign on I-5 would read. "A Conflict-Free Zone." Or perhaps Oregon, with its green, forward-thinking inhabitants, former governors exposing themselves to art, and our death with dignity laws, could light the torch. This could be a slogan custom made for license plates. Not "Live Free or Die," as is the motto for New Hampshire, but "Live Conflict Free or Die Trying." I see a proclamation by the governor. A photo op, something to be printed on the State of Oregon letterhead. Better yet, the whole Pacific Northwest— *Cascadia*—could adopt the philosophy. With its population of tree-hugging, salmon-kissing, Gaia-loving recyclers and the public relations aura it has achieved as a result, it's a natural. We're not weird; we're Northwesterners. We're ahead of the curve, that's all.

But wait. That path is fraught with conflict. In fact, that path may be the very *genesis* of conflict.

So instead, perhaps in a little house in the south of Eugene, one small family will struggle with the concept of no conflict, seeking every possible alternative in order to uplift the spiritual capacity of themselves and each other.

And maybe a member or two of that little family will discuss it with a member of another small family somewhere, and slowly, the light will take hold and spread, person to person, one to one, spirit touching spirit, like lighting candles. Calmly, peacefully, personally. The way the important information is to be passed, the way important jobs are to be done.

# Obi's Catapult

*Chika Unigwe*

Outside, the sun was an overfed stomach. Fat and round. A real beer-belly. Inside, the heat was suffocating. I could not concentrate on the lesson. I did not think anybody could for that matter. Not with that kind of sweltering killing heat. Our teacher, Mr. Okeke, kept pulling out his "was -white" handkerchief to wipe his very dark, very sweaty face. It was a Civic Studies lesson. We were being taught the duties of a good citizen. To be law abiding. I found that word amusing. Abiding, I mean. It sounded like a short man in an oversized *dashiki*. I let my mind wander out of this hot, hot class to the play field I could see from the open window, where *Abiding* struggled with his large gown. I swallowed the laughter that was threatening to bubble out, but it was too late. Mr. Okeke had noticed that my restless soul was not in his lesson.

"Sule," he bellowed, "give me another duty of a good citizen."

The entire class went quiet as my mind whirled through the textbook I had sat up with last night. It eventually came to my rescue. "A good citizen must be willing at all times to help the police, Sir."

Mr. Okeke reluctantly acknowledged that I had given a correct answer, and so I did not get punished for " not paying attention in class."

Mr. Okeke was my best friend's father, but he was as strict with me as with the next pupil. Each time I saw him at home, I could not reconcile the jovial man who played soccer with his son and me to the strict class teacher at school. Obi, his son, and I had been inseparable for nobody-knows-how-long.

We signed up for the same clubs and were both members of the school Boy Scout Movement. We tagged along to meetings together, feeling oh-so-important in our stiff green khaki shorts and shirts and very arrogant scarves tied around our necks. We marched side by side in the dust with the other scouts, chanting happily in unison,

Lord Baden Powell
He was a leader
Who used to wear khaki
Lord Baden Pooowell
He was a leader
Who used to wear khaaaki.

We went bird hunting together, as often as we could, our catapults safely tucked away in our pockets. Obi was very adept at catapulting. His skill earned him the nickname Baba catapult. A name he was very proud of, wearing it like a badge of honour. We had a salt-and-pepper relationship. Wherever you found one, the other was sure not to be far off.

I went round to Obi's family for birthday parties, christening parties, communion parties. I particularly liked going over there at Christmas. Then they had *jollof* rice which tasted like nothing I had ever tasted before. Pots overflowing with beef. Prepared and spiced in the way only Igbo people knew. And the special Christmas delicacy, goat head. He came round to our home for all our Muslim celebrations. We were forever in and out of each other's houses so that both sets of parents joked that their lives would be made easier if we decided to live in one of the two houses permanently. We would not have minded.

I do not now easily recollect the first time I suspected that something was wrong. Perhaps it was that Saturday afternoon when Mr. Okeke uncharacteristically told us off in a harsh tone for disturbing him with our "raucous laughter." He was the sort of man to use such words. Raucous. Boisterous. Debonair. Conflagration. I learnt all those from him. I used to joke with Obi that I was sure his father slept with *English Without Tears*. That was the only way I knew he could have learnt all those heavy-sounding words. I am sure we were very shocked at his taking offence at the amount of noise we made that day as it was the same amount of noise we made every day. What is that you measure noise in? Decibel? Thank you. We made the same decibel of noise as we did every other day. Mr. Okeke would be proud to hear me use that word. Decibel. It is just his type of word. We wondered why we were being scolded for doing nothing out of the ordinary.

Mrs. Okeke, Obi's mother, was also, in retrospect, rather quiet. She just sat in the sitting room, her oval face between her hands, a worried look crawling all over it. At that point neither Obi nor I took any notice of it. But as the days went by, we noticed changes in both our parents.

Obi's father stopped playing football with us, preferring to sit with his ears glued to his black transistor radio. In the classroom, he looked distracted, and we got off with a lot more mischief than we could have imagined. My mother, as my father was hardly around, eyed Obi with a look I had never seen before. Something akin to hostility.

Then we noticed that suddenly, there were riots around us. People shouting. Aggressive mobs waving placards. One day, I saw a man's head broken with a bottle and even as he begged for help, more people crowded in on him, beating him. His screams still haunt me. It was around that period my father told me matter-of-factly that the Sarduana had died. The Sarduana had been kidnapped and killed by a group of Igbo soldiers, he said, and I was to stop visiting Obi. I did not understand him. Could not. The Sarduana was dead. May Allah accept his soul. I was eight. Old enough to know that when someone died, it was a sad thing. And you were supposed to pray for the deceased's soul to find happiness in paradise. The Sarduana had been killed by some Igbo soldiers. I was eight. Old enough to understand that kidnapping and killing were sins against the Almighty Allah. But try as much as I could, I did not understand what all of that had to do with my best friend and I. Still, Father was authority with a capital "A," and I did not argue with him.

It was also around that period that I noticed that even though Obi and I still spoke in school, he had stopped coming around to our house. He told me that his father had told him that "it was not safe to visit the Hausa." Hausa, meaning my family and me. Obi, being more outspoken than I ever was, said he told his father that I was not just an Hausa, I was Sule, his friend. I often play out my imagination of this conversation. Mr. Okeke tells his son, " Obi, I have come to the decision that it is a risky affair to visit the Hausa" ( I am sure he would not have demeaned himself by putting it any other way). Obi tells him in his most stubborn voice, " But, Daddy, Sule is not Hausa. He is my best friend." Then Mr. Okeke tells him in his don't you-dare-argue-with-me teacher voice, " Well, I have made up my mind on this issue, and I will not brood any further argument."

I will always be grateful to Obi for standing up for me. I have never been able to have that kind of relationship with anybody else since Obi.

Obi, Obi, I still see him in my dreams. Every night I shut my eyes to sleep, I see him at our front door, in a pair of black trousers and a blue tee-shirt, the day he risked both my father's fearsome anger and his father's to tell me, his eyes full of salty tears, that they were moving back to the east. It was a Saturday afternoon, and they would be leaving the next day. His father had told him that the North was no longer safe for the Igbo. We both wondered why. I told him if it was not safe, I could try and convince my father to let them stay in our house. I can still hear myself, with all the sincerity of my age, my words rushing out like Danladi, the mad man's, "But but but but you do not have to go anywhere. Where is the east? You have never been there you do not know the people who will be your friend? What what what about the scouts? I will ask Baba if you can stay here I will beg him you'll see you'll be safe ."

Obi dug into his deep trouser pocket , brought out his catapult, his most prized possession and gave it to me. Sniffing and sucking in his tears, he told me, "Take, Sule. You'll keep it for me, eh? When we come back from the east, you'll give it back to me eh? And we'll go bird hunting together. I do not know anyone there. Who will I play with?"

Then he raced back to his house before either of my parents saw him. Or before his parents noticed his absence. I cried all day. I could not believe it. My best friend, going away. Leaving me. And he did not know when he would return. That day, my world ended.

Obi. Obi. Every night I shut my eyes, the stillness of the darkness is shattered into a million million pieces by the piercing, heart-stabbing screams I heard just before midnight from the Okeke's. It still sends shivers down the entire length of my back. A cocktail of voices letting out blood curdling cries and louder voices shouting, "Shut up! Shut up! Una be enemy. Enemy! Una don kill our Sarduana."

In the morning, before anyone could stop me, I ran over to Obi's. The door was open. I let myself in. And there they were. Bits and pieces. Two adult bodies. Limbs cut off and strewn all over the place. And a child's body, a body without a head. Obi's head was decapitated. His lifeless eyes stared at me from beside the fridge where his head had rolled. My mouth opened and did not stop shouting until a darkness enveloped me and the blue-and-white tiled floor rose up to meet me. A darkness I woke up from on my mother's bed, the family doctor hovering over me.

So many things happened that year. Like the civil war that started and lasted three years. A war I remember nothing about. I carry my own war in my heart, and it has not ended. I doubt it ever will. Obi's catapult is the first thing a visitor to my house notices. I have it hanging on the wall, right opposite my front door. It is a tribute to a great childhood friendship ruined by squabbling adults.

# Back to Country with Pulitzer

*Liam Rector*

I left here at eight
And returned at 75.
In between

I largely wasted America.
I married, had children,
Distinguished myself in a profession

Full of fools, becoming one myself,
As is the way
Of this (or, I suppose, of any other) world.

I missed
The Nobel but I did bring down
The Pulitzer. The weather,

The politics, the stars,
And my own small contribution
All lined up, and I got one.

So "Pulitzer" became my middle name
Before I came here, where no one seems
To care a whit about such things.

I failed at love.
That's where I truly fucked up.
I couldn't.

The women in this town
Are mostly severe, resentful
—The men bitter, disappointed.

A perfect place for my purposes.
I stay in a room
In the house of an old woman

Who doesn't want to have sex any more
And neither do I
So we do not

Trouble each other on that front,
Which is good.
I do like to drink.

I used to love to eat
But then I don't much
Give a shit

About any of that now.
The old woman sometimes says wistfully
God will soon be calling both of us

Back home, but as an agnostic
I don't believe that.
As an American,

I don't buy that.
I came here to retire from love,
To face my failure to love

As I attempted to face everything
Else before, and that
Is exactly what I am doing and doing

With the exactness I used to put in
To my work, for which I received the Pulitzer.

I hate a coward.

My son
Came here the other day and asked
Exactly when I might

Be coming back
And I sent him off without an answer.
The answer

Seems to be staying here,
Staying honestly here and coming to terms
With my greatest single failure.

My wife is dead. To me,
It seems I am left over
To eat a shit sandwich.

"Eat me," the world says,
now that I have lost my appetite.
We used to say "Eat me"

To each other in high school,
Another thing from which no one
Ever recovers. America likes to think

Every one can recover from every thing,
But about this,
Especially, America is wrong.

# In Hemingway Country

*Philip Raisor*

"Since you're going to Petoskey, take Hemingway's Michigan woods stories with you," Miss Wade said, her large left arm wafting toward the north exit of the hallway.

"Whose he," I asked, "when he's not heming his way home?"

"To no point," she said. "Always to no point."

I pointed toward the library. "That way?"

"And sign your name legibly, please," she said.

"Phil L-e-g-i-b-l-y." I said, moving swiftly beyond the finger-thumper aimed at my forehead.

Each August, for six years, our family nursed an undented Plymouth seven hundred miles up a two-lane highway from Muncie, Indiana, to Petosky, Michigan, where on Lake Douglas a small cabin became our escape from hay fever and the threat of polio. Tom, my brother, and I may have missed two weeks of daily basketball practice and hanging out at Tuhey pool, but we got instead a lake full of bass and pike and endless acreage of birch trees and rolling hills. We saw deer and raccoons, but we knew bears were just around a corner. Someone had seen a wildcat. We stomped at snakes; we fled hornets attacking from rotted logs. On the beach, Tom, Joe Beckner, and I raced each other, built sand stockades, and invented a game—a mixture of baseball, football, and swimming. Third base was the minnow box at the end of the pier; a home run was over a line full of the Caldwell sisters' bras and sweaters we called the end-zone. Joe spent a lot of time in the end-zone.

At sixteen, I had become, much to my embarrassment,

Miss Wade's prized student. "Think of it," she would say. "A basketball player who writes poetry." That wasn't true — I still thought poetry was for sissies, but Jack London and Ring Lardner, now that was another matter. "Never mind," Miss Wade would say. "Either way, you've got to understand the connection between books and the world." She would tell me over and over that all great writers read each other, that writing was a collective eye looking at the world. "Learn their techniques of seeing, practice it like basketball. Look through Hemingway's eyes." It made sense. I was Bob Cousy most of the time, especially driving the foul lane and passing behind the back to a hard-slicing wing man.

"All right, Coach Wade," I said to myself, chores done, and hands clean, "I'll read about Nick Adams, and then go to this Big Two-Hearted River country you want me to experience. I'll bring back a story for you." Tom was at an ROTC camp that summer, and Joe and his family had stopped coming. My mother and father shared quiet walks, the Detroit Tigers games on the radio, and hummed their own versions of Nat King Cole's "Mona Lisa." Left alone, I planned to read the Michigan woods stories first, and then make another plan. Just feel my way along. I started one sticky afternoon on the beach where Treva Caldwell was sunbathing. I read, imagined, and began to watch through Nick's eyes as his father in "Indian Camp" turned over the Indian's body to see his throat cut from ear to ear, just as Treva turned over on her back trying to cover her breast in time. I didn't see a thing I told her by dropping my head and reading harder. By the time Nick Adams had drunkenly stumbled through "The Three-Day Blow," I was intoxicated with Treva, sneaking peaks at her slightest movement as though she were a golden glass.

By the next morning, after a fantasy night, I had recovered. With permission, I packed the car with Hem's stories, my camera, notepad, fishing gear, wading boots, binoculars— everything I needed. In his "Up in Michigan" story, Hemingway writes, "Horton's Bay, the town, was only five houses on the main road between Boyne City and

Charlevoix." That was south of Petoskey, and I knew that if I stayed on Route 31, I could retrace Nick's territory by noon and then, backtracking, head north of Pellston for the rest of the afternoon. By the next day, I would be across the Mackinaw City bridge, through the Hiawatha National Forest, and onto the dirt roads that ran all the way through the Upper Peninsula to Lake Superior.

But south of Petoskey was no longer "up the road" and "down the road" farming country. It had become city-fied, with too many signs, stores, cars, and trucks that would stalk you from behind. I wanted the Hemingway of swamp mud, grasshoppers, open fires, and the sound a fence makes when you crawl over it. I turned around, and though I know I tempted every cop on the side of the road, by nightfall I got what I wanted. Tomorrow, I would fish in the Big-Two Hearted River.

In the middle of the night, fetal in the back seat of the Plymouth on the berm of a road, dreaming of meadows and Treva and trout, I was ripped awake by godawful screams and the rocket-roar of a revved-up truck. Out the back window I could see waving arms and beer cans ricocheting off road signs and flags about Lamda Chi something. I ducked down as a spotlight sped past, spun around, and then fired into the front seat. "Anything in there," somebody yelled. Dirt and rocks spun against the front door, and the rioters were off again. Tucked on the floorboard, I imagined them coming back, pulling me out of a busted side window, cutting off arms, tossing pieces to the wolverines, burying car parts in the undergrowth. I was afraid, but the fear was not fresh or deep. I was even almost ready to step out and confront them *and me* if they came back.

They did—in a wild, swerving rush up to the side door. In unison six of them leaned over like swine at a trough, spaced a foot apart, and on command pissed from roof to tires, hood to trunk, as if they wanted to tear paint from metal. Not all the windows were tight. As rocks spun again against the car, I gripped the door handle, but my hand, a totally separate thing, warmly wet and sticky, leaped back and wiped itself against my pants. I didn't know, or care, what they were singing as the truck bounced back down the road like a chandelier in a dust storm.

In the morning, stiff-necked and smelling like an outhouse, I realized I had dreamed, off and on, about my hand in a grave, putrefying. My mind said, "So What! You wiped it in mud and leaves. Forget it. You're going fishing." Still, I felt queasy, as though I had gotten bruised ribs or a cut lip in practice.

I smelled the dew and felt the morning sun hot on my back. The grasshoppers were sluggish as I walked along and plopped them in a glass jar just as Nick had done. Yes, that's what I was here for. To walk in Nick Adams shoes, to see with his eyes. I would try. I started. Story in hand, I read, "Nick leaned back against a stump and slipped out of the pack harness. Ahead of him, as far as he could see, was the pine plain. The burned country stopped off at the left with the range of hills. On ahead, islands of dark pine trees rose out of the plain." I saw that, too. I saw stumps and insects and two jack pines. The more I walked and read, and the more I saw that little if anything had changed from Hemingway's pages to my meadow-wet pants, I realized the lines between past and present had been broken. I was in his story. He was in my life. Fact and fiction and history were all one and this moment was real to me. It seemed that I understood why I read. I could live in a broader world. I could be more than myself.

I stopped next to a fallen elm tree and listened to the chirr, twitter, and scurry of unseen life. The burr-grass barely moved in the breeze. Looking back, I saw I had meandered in the open field, searching maybe for the end of the meadow or maybe even walking aimlessly, in no hurry, toward a trout stream. Maybe I would just sit for awhile, look back, and think of Treva. The dew was drying out and my path was disappearing. In a few more minutes that part of the trip would be gone, except in my mind.

Then I remembered I had Hem's "Big Two-Hearted River" in my hand and it was his plan I was following. He said to look ahead, listen to the sounds of the river current rushing through the copse of trees ahead of you.

"Nick felt awkward and professionally happy with all his equipment hanging from him. The grasshopper bottle swung against his chest. In his shirt the breast pockets bulged against him with the lunch and his fly book."

I realized I was hungry, monstrously so, and foolishly had brought nothing along, not even a Snickers. I thought I had everything. What had I been thinking? Hunger was worse than a putrefying hand. I knew right then the rest of my adventure would be shortened.

I hurried toward the river, fumbling with my camera, realizing I wanted to take a few pictures. The pace of moving, thinking, seeing suddenly accelerated, and when I stopped at the bank—book in one hand, camera in the other, and the jar of grasshoppers in my armpit—I knew that Nick's entry into the water wouldn't be mine. "He stepped into the stream. It was a shock. His trousers clung tight to his legs. His shoes felt the gravel. The water was a rising cold shock." I felt nothing. I was not relaxed, happy. I was not in the Hemingway *moment*. My thinking and my body were in two different places.

I saw the other bank and kept sloshing toward it. Yet I kept wanting to stop or slow down. Something was leaving me.

Then, literally, I slipped on a stone, and it was all over. Book, camera, and grasshoppers went flying, and I plunged to my knees. *Now,* the water was icy cold. *Now,* my skin shriveled in terror. I had no choice but to stop, adjust, gather myself. I was in the Big Two-Hearted River, all alone, and all around me the gnarled land and fractured logs were unmoved, unchanged by my disturbance.

Crawling out of the river, I knew I had not seen trout leap into the air or "dive down into the light, under the logs." I had not seen what Hemingway and Nick had—fine trout laid out on the grass. But cold and hungry, I had seen six guys, standing like pigs in a row. I was no longer Nick or Hem in their story, but me in mine—and I wanted a hard grip on a slaughtering knife. I knew that would pass, but it's what I saw and felt. I was sure that would be the truth I would have to tell.

So I decided right there that I would go back to Miss Wade and thank her for the opportunity to connect life and art in her way. But I'd have to tell her I couldn't see much point in practicing someone else's seeing. What I could do though, I would say, with great affection and at some distance from her gifted finger, was try to catch my own trout in my own stream if that'd do any good. Then I'd duck.

# New Roads

*Natalie Olsen*

Trimmed by tractor, not by sheep
the pastures now are lawns.
All trace and smells have blown away
except for tufts of wool on fences
felted by years of itchy ewes.

Coyotes still howl their threats at night
but stay away. It's the *day* sounds now
we fear…the trucks, the roads,
the people
filling up the land.

# Mrs. Ryan's Last Lesson

*Dorothy Read*

South Whidbey High School sparkled after its summer scrubdown. Reflections bounced off the polished concrete floors; lockers gleamed under their new layer of Falcon blue epoxy paint. Room 205 was at September ready on this, the first day of my last year of teaching, ever. A pretty room, with flower vines stretching around the walls, painted over the years by myriad freshmen—an English garden for an English classroom. Blue blossoms, pink, lavender, yellow, with an occasional whimsical insect and the odd fairy here and there, little Tinkerbells added by a student who wrote lovely fantasy.

My last first day, I was thinking wistfully, when my last first student walked in. First he filled the doorway, then he filled the room.

"Good morning, Mrs. Ryan—it is Mrs. Ryan, isn't it? I haven't had the pleasure of meeting you yet. I'm Barton. I love English, and I know I'm going to love this class. By the way, I hope you like the old movie classics..." He extended a vast paw. I shook it and nodded an awed greeting. Still talking, he selected a desk to wear, and his cheerfulness effervesced, surrounding himself and me, and bubbling up around the other students as they entered the room. They took him in stride.

"Hey, Barton," they replied to his greetings and high fives, and then they turned away to clump up in their own social circles, none of which seemed to include Barton. His good spirits, however, were unflagging.

The kid was big—big girth, big smile, big mouth, constant mouth. Every time my eyes brushed third row, front, the mouth was in motion. He was a conversation pit unto himself, distracting no one, it seemed, but me.

"Barton, are you with me?"

"Yes, Mrs. Ryan, I swear I am." Enthusiastic. Courteous. The first assignment belied his oath.

"This is the best piece of writing I ever failed," I wrote next to the "F" at the top of the page.

He received it with a great, agreeable grin and tucked it away in his book bag.

I found a moment in the bustling classroom to talk to him personally. "Barton, I see some nice writing in that piece," I began.

"Thanks, Mrs. Ryan," he beamed, lively brown eyes warmly acknowledging the accolade.

"But, uh," I stumbled into the next phase of the comment, "it wasn't what I asked for."

"Oh, really?" Astonished.

"Really. Do you still have the assignment sheet?"

He unzipped the voluminous book bag, and the English assignment lay near the top of a thin layer of course syllabi and class rules. He smiled with triumphant pleasure at the quick find.

I pressed on. "I was looking for something creative, but it's supposed to be based on your lecture notes about William Shakespeare."

"Oh." Thoughtful. "I guess I missed the William Shakespeare part."

"I guess you did. But the story about the two brothers in a duck blind is very well done. Save it to work on later, when we're doing short fiction."

"You bet, Mrs. Ryan." The expansive smile was back. The "F" hadn't made a dent. "You may redo the assignment."

"I may?" Grateful. "I'll do that." But he didn't.

The next assignment was a group effort: a mock Elizabethan newspaper. Each student was required to research an event of the period and write it as a news article in the language of Shakespeare. Barton's group tried very hard to eject him.

"Mrs. Ryan, he never does his work," they complained in confidence. Barton had been building his reputation since Kindergarten.

"I'm sure Barton will come through for you. After all, this is high school," I reminded them. They grumbled, but agreed to give him a chance.

Instead of a researched article, Barton created a full-page ad for lances guaranteed to meet their marks in the joust. His newspaper group was fuming, and they insisted I lean on him.

"Barton, the lance ad is very creative."

"Thanks, Mrs. Ryan. I'd hoped you would like it." Delighted.

"Uh, it would be a nice feature for the newspaper, but you still owe your group a researched article."

"Researched article?" Surprised, shocked.

"Can you find the assignment sheet?" I asked, and before long it churned up from the depths of the book bag.

The misunderstanding was resolved, the newspaper group placated, and for the rest of the class period Barton was busy searching the world wide web for a scoop on the defeat of the Spanish Armada. "I'll have it ready tomorrow," he vowed with sincerity that no one could doubt.

The next day, with a flourish, he produced his manuscript—an insightful piece on the irony of campaign reform. His newspaper group members were not amused.

"Barton," I began. "This is a very mature piece of writing."

"No kidding, Mrs. Ryan?" Pleased, proud.

"But, uh, it has nothing to do with Elizabethan England."

"Elizabethan England?" Startled, stunned.

Their newspaper was put to bed, short one researched article, and the group was in solidarity about never working again with Barton. He didn't seem to mind too much, and his full-page ad was a crowd favorite when the newspapers were shared.

The year was a long series of lasts—the last set of short story posters, the last class poetry book, the last debate on whether George did the right thing by Lennie. Well-meaning colleagues marked the year's progression. "Hey, Lil— one quarter down, only three to go!"

...two to go. ...one to go. "How does it feel?"

I would grin the expected response, but by mid-April it felt like someone was pushing hard on my shoulders, shoving them toward the ground. I began to wonder what I would be when I was no longer a teacher. Then Barton would fizz into the room and dilute gravity.

"Mrs. Ryan, do you like *Fiddler on the Roof?*"

"I love *Fiddler on the Roof!*"

"No kidding! Watch this!" Within moments we were caught up in "If I Were a Rich Man," parading, shaking our shoulders and snapping our fingers, Chaim Topol style. The next day we were singing, "Tradition... tradition..." And the next, "Sunrise, Sunset," complete with dewy eyes. I sang a gravelly harmony to Barton's exuberant melody, carried somewhere between the tenor he was leaving and the bass he was becoming.

Students gawked at first, as they filed into the room, barely awake at 7:30 in the morning.

I would hear whispers. "Oh, man, Barton's at it again." "What's with Mrs. Ryan?" "She's acting all. . .weird." "Way weird!" But then they came to expect a spectacle, and some even joined in.

When we had exhausted all the good songs in *Fiddler on the Roof, Music Man,* and *Carousel,* Barton took up drumming, and students filed in to the sound of dueling drums, their teacher pounding away at the lectern in answer to Barton's desk tattoo. One morning Scott uncorked his trumpet. The next day Charlie hauled his guitar into class. Others brought their instruments, and the rest joined Barton and me in the percussion section. We had an early morning jazz band that brought students to the door. The principal occasionally came to the door, too, wondering if adult supervision was needed in the classroom. I would wave at him between sets and he would leave, still wondering. Once the bell rang, we abandoned the jam and turned our attention to English. No amount of bad news about grades seemed to quash Barton's upbeat spirit. All year his grade hovered between critical and flatline. He accepted one dreadful grade after another with smiling good grace, a collection of D's and F's padding the deep recesses of the book bag. Even the creative short story had gone awry, the duck blind abandoned for a collection of annotations on Betty Davis films. By the end of the year, he was still on the endangered species list.

"Barton, it is going to make me sick if I have to flunk you."

"Oh, gosh, Mrs. Ryan, don't feel bad." Concerned, sympathetic. "This is a great class," he added, to console me.

"The point is, you don't have to flunk it."

"I don't?" Attentive, interested.

"You have a final project and a final exam left to do. If you get a C on both, you can pass the class."

"Hmmm." Meditative. He stroked his chin in a dramatic pose. Humphrey Bogart, I think.

"So why don't you get out that final project assignment sheet?" Déjà vu. How many times had we performed this scene?

Sheets of paper in varying stages of fermentation erupted from the bag until, at last, the final assignment turned up. It called for a well-supported persuasive essay: 1,500 words in standard manuscript form, complete with footnotes and bibliography. Two weeks of golden class time had already been devoted to the project.

"So far so good," I said, smoothing out the abused sheet of paper. "Now show me what you've done so far." I was hoping to see the campaign reform essay, resurrected.

Nothing came forth. Students nearby snickered.

"So how much have you done on this assignment?" I felt my thermostat rising.

"Well, actually, nothing." Regretful.

In the thirty-eight teaching years preceding this moment, I had never turned an expletive loose on a kid. They had rattled off the rafters at home, but none had ever slid out in the classroom. Until now.

"Then what have you been doing for the last two freaking weeks?" Well, I meant to say freaking, but it rhymed with plucking. I froze, waiting for every principal I'd ever worked for to materialize and fire me, eight days short of the end of my career.

Twenty-seven of twenty-eight students also froze, absorbing the reality that the oldest, grey-headedest, grandmotherliest teacher on staff had just popped the F-word. Barton, however, was unfazed.

"The fact is, Mrs. Ryan, I've been writing my screenplay!" His eyes glowed as he tugged a sleek black 3-ring binder out of the black hole of his book bag. "You want to see it? I got the idea when we read *To Kill a Mockingbird*. And then Eli Wiesel's *Night* really got me thinking..."

He chatted on as I turned pages of what appeared to be a well-formatted, superbly written, bonafide screen drama.

"Barton, how long have you been working on this?"

"Oh, gosh, for weeks. It's taking a long time, you see, because I've had to do so much research..."

"You've been doing research?" I felt an epiphany coming on.

"Tons! Look at the bibliography—four pages!" Cheerful, proud.

My legs turned to Jell-O, and I sagged into the empty desk next to him.

"Mrs. Ryan, are you all right?"

"That depends upon whether you can make a logical connection between this..." I waggled the black notebook, "...and a 1,500-word persuasive essay."

The entire class, on board and eager for the answer, leaned forward, collectively. Barton reflected for the briefest instant in a Gregory Peck attitude, and then recovered his momentum.

"Well, I'll tell you the honest truth, I'm just fed up with hate crimes, aren't you? I mean, I don't see much difference between some of the stuff that's going on now—right here in our country!—and the stuff the Nazis did during the holocaust. So my play shows what happens when we keep our mouths shut and let these bullies get away with..."

The play was about a gay college student who had always wanted to be a teacher. He was targeted by so-called "patriots," harassed, and finally beaten to death. Barton's classmates pitched in to help him perform the drama. Through those last few days of my teaching career, my students and I watched Barton's story take life. We lived the young man's pain and fear as he received hate mail and threatening phone calls. We felt helpless as he sought protection, but was turned away by the college security and law enforcement agencies. We endured humiliation as his straight friends denounced him rather than get involved. We suffered disappointment as his gay friends distanced themselves out of fear. We wept as he died, finally, at the hands of thugs who could have been stopped at many points along the tragic story line. At the end, Barton's classmates declared the play—and the playwright—awesome, the ultimate tribute.

Barton swept through the sixty-minute final exam in thirty minutes. He left the class in pretty much the same manner he had entered it, except this time he was welcome in the social circles.

"Mrs. Ryan," he said, pumping my hand so vigorously I felt I was being wagged, "this is the best English class I ever had. I learned sooooooo much!"

Me too, Barton, me too.

He passed English with a solid B.

# Wolf Love

*Victory Lee Schouten*

I read,
most whales
and most wolves

choose life mates,
loving ferociously forever.

I see
some men
and some women

choose pain and blame,
loving gingerly at best.

I want wolf love
with you.

Wolf love, with you.

# Things That Go Bump in the Lake

*Rowena Williamson*

Polly stepped awkwardly into the rubber contraption and giggled. She waded out, holding up the float tube, trying to maintain her balance and not tip over. The lake floor shelved down, and she floated wader clad legs and finned feet in the water.

"Whee," she whispered.

She had ordered everything (Creek Company U-Boat 2000 Super Combo, Complete with Free Fins and Air Pump, and Guide-Weight Stockingfoot Waders, Toughest 5mm Wader Available!) from Cabela's Online Catalog. Her husband had no idea she had ordered them. It was her secret. Lord knew, since Evan had retired she had few of them.

Fins moving gently, she maneuvered away from shore. Every time she drove by Pass Lake, she had watched the fishermen floating over the surface, rods whipping back and forth, at peace.

*Why not,* she had thought, *just float the day away? Do you have to have a fishing pole?*

There seemed no reason not to float away from demands of husband, calls for her to volunteer for everything on the island, calls from adult children still in need of mothering. Peace, afloat on her own little island, with handy pockets in the tube and waders that held, not the extra flies, tackle and various fishing gear they were made for, but sun screen, a lunch purchased at a gourmet deli, a small bottle of wine, and a brand new, never-read-by-anyone mystery novel. Her commuter mug full of latte rested in an open pocket of her waders. Polly placed her sun hat firmly in place on her graying hair, secured the hat's cord under her chin, then glided, small ripples in her wake, across mirror—like waters to the west side, where trees grew down to hang over the lake.

The sun warmed her back while cool water swirled around her waders and liners. Bird song and the occasional sound of a car on the highway that ran by the lake broke the morning silence. Polly tipped her head back to watch an eagle gliding over her. Bliss.

She pulled her book out of a pocket and her mug of latte from another. The Charles Todd mystery sent her to post-World War One England.

The brush of something on her cheek startled her. Polly looked up to see she had drifted near the bank, and small branches had halted the tube. Trees formed a shadowy cave in front of her. She back pedaled with her fins and pulled away from the bank, bumping into something behind her. From the corner of her eye she saw the side of another float tube.

"Oh, I'm sorry, I hope I didn't..." She turned the tube and stared at Elroy Vance, not her favorite neighbor. Elroy specialized in building huge ugly houses, even suing the county for the privilege of erecting them on wetlands and bluffs. Polly, chairperson of the Stop Vance Committee, narrowed her eyes at the sleeping Vance, his rod propped against the side of the tube, his Tilley hat tipped over his eyes. Polly had never seen him so still. Vance's usually florid face was gray.

Funny...

Polly looked closer. "Uh oh," she said.

Her first thought was, *Evan is going to find out about the equipment, and he's going to be pissed.* Her second thought was *Oh, boy, that's a hole in his head. That's blood.*

It *was* a hole, right in the side of Vance's head under the rakishly tilted hat. Blood ran down from the hole into his collar. Polly knew she didn't want to look at the other side of his head. She had read enough mysteries to have an idea what that would look like.

"Okay, okay, what do I do? The cell phone, right, in the car," Polly muttered. She looked around; no other fishermen were on the lake, no other cars but her own in the parking lot—wait, there was Vance's big Humvee hidden under trees to the left of the lot. How had she missed it? She realized her mind was stumbling over things that were pointless right then. Of course those thoughts kept her from remembering that hole in Vance's head.

Polly started paddling toward the landing, glancing over her shoulder occasionally to make sure Vance was still there. Her book had fallen overboard near his tube and her Amazon.com commuter mug bobbed in her wake. Should she recover her things? Were they evidence?

"Oh, God," she muttered, remembering the last County Commissioners' meeting where she had waved maps at Vance and shouted that he was ruining the island with his plan to build a recreational development on the north end. He had laughed at her and she had yelled after him, "You haven't heard the last from me!"

As she pulled herself up on the bank in front of her car she looked back again at the form bobbing near the trees. She tripped getting out of the float tube, managed to pull her fins off, ran to the car, then back to the tube to pull out her keys. Her hand shook as she tried to put the key in the lock, then the world spun around her.

Polly crouched on the ground, leaning against the car, head between her knees and told herself, "Breathe deep, from your belly. Breathe. Clear your mind." Her yoga teacher would have been proud.

Standing again on shaking legs, she opened the car, pulled out the phone, took another deep breath, and called 911.

"Hello, yeah, um, this is Polly Russell. I'm at Pass Lake, and there's a dead man in a float tube. I didn't shoot him, I just found him. Yeah, I'll stay here. I didn't disturb the crime scene. It's water."

Evan next. She had to call Evan.

"Hi, honey. Look, there's a little problem. Yeah, I'm sorry I didn't leave a note. No, the car is fine. I'm at Pass Lake. I was wondering, do you think you might come up here?" Polly realized her voice was quavering. "Elroy Vance...he's out in Pass Lake in a float tube, and he's been killed, and I bumped into him. Well, yeah, I was in a float tube, too. Evan, I'll explain everything when you get here, I think I hear the police coming."

Polly hung up before Evan could ask more questions. She sighed. It would take at least fifteen minutes for him to get here. She hoped the police wouldn't have her in hand-cuffs before then. She leaned against the car and wondered if it would be okay to drink her wine.

Lights flashing, a County Sheriff's car pulled up beside Polly's car and two men stepped out. The driver was the sort of officer that made one think of dank Southern jails and guys named Bubba. Though he was probably in his early twenties, he had the sort of soft fat that spoke of too many Big Macs. His neck and head were the same circumference and a uniform pink. He had shaved his head, and his eye-lashes and eyebrows were so pale they blended in with the rest of him. His eyes, pale blue, stared at her with little inter-est. His name pin read Dwayne Brinker.

The other man walked toward her and smiled. Tall, lean, with a graying moustache, he looked every inch the sheriff.

"Ms Russell? I'm sheriff Jim Andrews."

Realizing she had been staring, Polly gave a tentative smile and nodded.

"Now, then, where is the body? Dwayne, pay attention."

The younger man was scanning the lake with binocu-lars. "I don't see nothing," he muttered.

"Well, he's out there, by the trees," Polly said, irritated. "I wouldn't have called otherwise."

Brinker gave her a scornful glance. Polly read it as *Dizzy Old Woman*.

"Sheriff, it's Elroy Vance, and he's been shot."

"What's that stuff floating in the water by the trees?" Brinker asked.

Polly gulped. "It...it's my book and latte mug. I guess I dropped them."

Another scornful look from Brinker. Polly scowled back at him.

"Now, then, Ms Russell, can you tell me what happened? Dwayne, take notes."

"Well, I was out there..."

"Fishing?" Andrews looked over at Polly's float tube.

"Um, no, actually, I was reading."

Brinker snorted. "Reading? With a latte?"

Polly flushed. "What's the matter, can't you hear me? Yes, I was floating around with a latte and reading a book. A book, you know?"

"Now, Ms Russell, you were out in your float tube, reading, having your latte." Andrews' patient voice broke in. "And then what happened?"

"Well, I wasn't paying attention, and I floated into the trees over there, and I sort of back pedaled, and bumped into something behind me. When I turned around, I saw it was Elroy Vance, and thought he was asleep, then I saw the hole in his head and came back to shore and called you."

A car came screeching up. "Oh, and then I called my husband. That's him."

Evan boiled out of the car and ran toward the three of them.

"Polly, what the hell is going on? What have you done?"

"Sir, your wife hasn't done anything," the sheriff said. "She's found a body and now she's answering my questions. Dwayne, call the water rescue squad and have them get over here."

"What if she's messed up the murder site?" Dwayne hitched up his belt over his belly.

Andrews sighed. "Dwayne, it's *water.*"

Dwayne blushed and went to the patrol car.

Evan, his face nearly as red as Dwayne's, said, "Polly, what the hell were you doing here?"

"I was floating, dear. I was floating and reading and

drinking my latte, and I ran into Elroy Vance, and he was dead."

Evan sat down on a log and stared at her. "Okay, now, where did you get the equipment, and why? You don't even fish. And...*Elroy Vance?* The guy you threatened at the commissioners' meeting?"

"Excuse me?" Sheriff Andrews said.

"I ordered them from Cabela's. I thought it would be a great way to, well, get away."

"From me?" Evan asked, looking hurt.

"Excuse me?" the sheriff repeated.

"From everything, Honey. I just haven't had a whole lot of time to myself, and when we decided not to take a vacation this year, well, I just bought this stuff and decided to take day vacations on the lake. And then I found Elroy my first time out."

"Mrs. Russell! Please explain about your threat to Mr. Vance."

Polly looked reproachfully at her husband. Really, he shouldn't have said anything about that.

"Elroy wants—wanted—to build a resort in an area that's environmentally unsound. My group is protesting it, and I just warned him he hadn't heard the last from me. But I didn't...I wouldn't do anything like that."

The deputy returned. "They're on their way." He cast a suspicious glance at Polly.

The four of them stood, staring out at the lake.

After the water rescue squad had gotten their Zodiac in the water and the peaceful lake was disturbed by the roar of its motor, Andrews drew Polly aside.

"Now, then, Mrs. Russell, who are the others in your group?"

"There are about twenty of us, five or six who are really active, and I swear to you, I can't think of anyone who'd actually shoot Elroy."

"Can you give me their names?" Andrews asked.

"Yeah. George Anderson—he's the head of the environmental group, SOI—Save Our Island—and his wife Libby.

But they're on vacation in Alaska. Bill Pearson. Bill is really anti-gun. And me. And Annalee Metzger. And Annalee is..."

"What?" Andrews asked.

Over Andrews' shoulder Polly watched the Zodiac bump gently against the float tube that carried Elroy Vance.

"It's nothing, I guess. But you know her, don't you? Everyone on the island knows Annalee. She's been writing an environmental watchdog column for years in the Tribune. And she's an old lady, I mean really old." Polly gulped and couldn't meet the sheriff's stare.

"And?" the sheriff prompted.

"Oh, God, I feel just awful even mentioning it. She stands to lose more than anyone. Her property is next to the proposed development, and runoff from construction could destroy her lavender farm and maybe even her well. It's just..."

Evan said, "Annalee Metzger is ninety five. She couldn't —"

"Please, sir, just let your wife talk."

Polly shook her head. "He's right...she couldn't. It's just that Annalee said she wouldn't be able to live her last days in her own home if Vance got the okay. And she does use a gun for rabbits in her garden." Polly looked helplessly at the sheriff and her husband. "I shouldn't have said anything. I'm sure it's not Annalee. She's a dear friend of mine and I'd never forgive myself if I've caused trouble for her." Tears ran down Polly's cheeks.

Evan put his arms around her. "Can we go home, Sheriff?"

Andrews nodded. "Yeah. Mrs. Russell, I'll go talk to Annalee. Don't worry, I'll do all I can for her—if it is her."

"Wait, can I go with you? Evan, I really need to talk to her, to apologize."

Andrews nodded. "She's not really in trouble. But it could comfort her to see a friendly face."

Evan said, "I'll follow you. Take off your waders and I'll throw everything in the car."

Polly climbed in beside Sheriff Andrews. "Annalee is such a dear, and she cares so much about the island. I've worked with her on all sorts of projects, and she's raised money to purchase land to keep it from being developed. I don't know why I thought of her gun."

Andrews looked over at her. "Free association, probably. Not many local people have guns these days. I wouldn't worry, Mrs. Russell. I've known her most of my life, and she's a tough old lady, but she *is* an old lady, and old ladies don't go around shooting people." He chuckled at the thought.

They drove through farmland bordered by tall firs till Andrews turned off onto a rough gravel road between two fields of blooming lavender. Polly rolled down her window. Poor old Annalee.

Annalee's house had changed little since her great-grand-father had built it in the mid-nineteenth century. White walls shone in the sunlight, and the green trim had been newly painted.

Annalee Metzger, clad in rubber boots and overalls, her white hair a halo around her tanned face, came out onto her front porch as the two cars pulled up, a dust cloud following them.

"Well Jimmy Andrews—and Polly! What brings you here?" she asked as they stepped up on the porch. "Did Vance call you when he swam out of the lake?"

Evan joined them, and Annalee clicked her tongue and gestured them inside.

The hallway was crowded with baskets and smelled of lavender. Beside one basket stood a rifle with a scope on it.

Andrews stopped beside it and asked, "Annalee, what makes you think Vance had to swim out of Pass Lake?"

"Well, I guess I shouldn't have done it, but he just made me so damn mad. He came over yesterday and offered to buy me out, said I was too old to try to run the farm, even with my son's help. Roger's seventy, and he wants to retire and told Vance so. Anyhow, I'd seen him several times in the early morning fishing in the lake. I always suspected he went early so he could get away with breaking the catch and release law. So I took my gun down there before light this morning, and when he got into the water I shot his float tube and got out of there fast. I knew he could get to shore. I just wanted to make him think about what he was planning to do. How did he know it was me?"

The sheriff sighed. "Well, now, Annalee. I'm afraid you aimed a little high, maybe about two, two and a half feet."

Polly reached out and touched Annalee's shoulder. "I'm so sorry..."

Annalee looked at Polly. "About what, dear?"

"I was out on the lake, and I found him, and Sheriff Andrews asked about other people in the Stop Vance movement, and, well..."

Annalee patted Polly's hand absently. "Is he dead?"

Andrews said, "Yeah, I'm afraid so."

Annalee drew in a deep breath and slumped a little, suddenly an old, old woman. "Well, then, I reckon I'd better change clothes and come with you, Jimmy. You better take my gun. I guess I've gotten too old to shoot straight. I sure am sorry I've caused you trouble."

Andrews patted her back as she turned. "Now, Annalee, don't you worry any; we'll straighten this all out and you'll be back home in no time. I'll bet we can even find someone to help with the farm."

Annalee slowly climbed the stairs, looked over her shoulder at Andrews and Evan examining the gun, and then smiled at Polly.

# King Of The Butterflies

*Christopher Howell*

In the last days of the reign of John II Casimer,
King of Poland, it was decreed that two million
butterflies, 100,000 for each of his years
upon the throne, should be captured and sent up
to God, an offering of the Earth's bounty in praise
of His role in the establishment of true regality.
Thousands of peasants were set to the construction
of nets and the most delicate snares so that each
lovely animal could be brought perfect and alive
to the grace of sacrifice. Blackguards and blasphemers
were released from gaol, promised royal pardons
and gold should each deliver within seven days 1,000
of the brilliant fliers to Korbecki, Chancellor
of the Realm, Keeper of Keys and Lists.

Those who brought moths by mistake were impaled
and left to die screaming outside the Palace of Justice.
Those who brought dead or damaged goods were forced
to eat them, then to wrestle the King's bull, Njok,
whose hoofs were razors and who had never been bested.

Frequently the butterflies were brought in little cages
such as one might build to house a cricket or a god
of those slim shadows wavering in out-of-the-way elbows
of a pond-side path. An entire corner of the King's
garden, jammed with nectar-bearing blossom, was netted
to contain the fluttering magnificence which, as the insects
grew in number, came more and more to resemble

a single dazzling existence, moving in undulant, serpentine
iridescence below the terrace where the King would
sometimes stand rubbing his hands as he watched.

On the seventh day the counters declared their collection
still 176,314 butterflies shy of numerical fulfillment,
which fact the Chancellor tremblingly reported to His
Majesty, who forgave him this failure and awarded him
three hours to make up the short-fall
or else.

Korbecki ran from the presence and pressed
virtually everyone he met into his personal service,
sending flocks of searchers into the meads
laden with cages and nets and nectarly enticements. The last
pennies of his fortune he spent bribing the counters (a small
army of dwarves in lace gloves) to announce that a sufficiency
of butterflies had at last been obtained. They took his money
but declined. Peasant after peasant returned with single
white admirals, or with woodland graylings almost
too small to be counted.

"What is happened, dear God?" Korbecki pleaded aloud,
at which words an old chandler approaching with a large
spotted fritillary in a reed cage said, "Excellency,
you have already nearly all the butterflies in Poland.
Would you have us bring Russian butterflies? Lithuanian
butterflies? Butterflies who do not even know our language?
Of course you would not! But happily, Sire," he said
smiling, "I have captured the King of all Polish butterflies!"
Korbecki briefly considered having the man dismembered
and fed to the royal goldfish, but instead, taking a wild chance,
bent to the little cage and spoke to the fritillary, "Oh
small but mighty one, how may I find, within the meadow
of an hour, 170,000 of your most beautiful brethren?"
And in a melodious voice the King of Polish butterflies
replied, "I have heard of this foolishness and, as you see,
have myself been caught in it. If you release me, I will send
what you desire, but this sacrifice," he said with the shadow
of a laugh, "will be quite impossible and will cost you
your life."

"If you do not send them," said the suddenly weary
and no longer astonished by anything Korbecki, "my life is forfeit,
in any case." And he opened the cage saying, "Gather them, then."
And the bright creature flew off toward the forests.

Twenty minutes later a blizzard of color blew out of a cloud
and descended on the gatherers who plucked them, tenderly, every
one. And when the last painted lady was tipped into the enclosure,
huge crowds assembled to watch the sacrifice proceed
and were stunned into silence by the beauty of the swarm,
by the fragrance of the wind which two million sets of wings
brought to them. And when the King of Poland ordered Korbecki
to torch the enclosure, to send up to God the splendor or his
Kingdom's butterflies in the form of smoke, Korbecki
wept and could not be brought to do it and the King had him torn
and eaten by wild pigs. And when the next chancellor also refused,
the King had molten lead poured into his ears and anus. When
a third still refused, the King raged and took up the torch
himself and marched to the immense cauldron of wheeling color,
and, finding even himself unable to take so much beauty
from the world, he cut the netting and the butterflies surged up
like an explosion of confetti, like all the world's flowers
flung into the arms of God. And the King perceived
that this tribute was acceptable and complete

It was June 1, in the year 1668. The next day John II Casimir
abdicated the throne and was carried off weeping and broken
in a cage of silver roses.

# The Editors

**Marian Blue** has published hundreds of articles, essays, poetry, fiction and interviews (most recently in: *Drive, women's true stories of the open road*—Seal Press anthology; *Eureka Literary Magazine, Snowy Egret, Raven Chronicles; Mankato Poetry Review; Lynx Eye*—forthcoming). She edits for One World Journeys and Blue & Ude Writers Services, she teaches for Skagit Valley College and Writers Digest Schools. (www.blueudewritersservices.com)

**Celeste Mergens** writes and edits from Whidbey Island, Washington where she is founder and director of the Whidbey Island Writers Association, which sponsors the nationally acclaimed Whidbey Island Writers Conference. An avid supporter and promoter of writers, her own publishing credits include *Creations Magazine* and *Parent's Magazine* as well as several produced plays.

# The Contributors

**Ann Adams** is a Texas native who moved to Whidbey Island in 1982. Her stories have appeared in *Beneath the Rain Shadow III* and *Take Our Words for Whidbey*, anthologies published by the Whidbey Writers Group.

**Kelli Russell Agodon's** poems have appeared in the *Seattle Review, Rattapallax, Parnassus, River Oak Review, Calyx,* and other publications. She is a 2000 Artist Trust GAP grant recipient and the Poetry Editor of the literary journal Margin: Exploring Modern Magical Realism. To read more of her work, visit www.geocities.com/agodon.

**Brian Ames** writes from the Puget Sound area of Washington state. His work appears in *Glimmer Train Stories, The Massachusetts Review, Sweet Fancy Moses* and *Weber Studies*, as well as several other magazines and online. Pocol Press of Virginia published his story collection, *Smoke Follows Beauty*, in 2002.

**Diane Averill** has published two full-length collections of poetry: *Branches Doubled Over With Fruit*, in 1991, University of Florida Press; *Beautiful Obstacles*, in 1998, Blue Light Press. Litany was published in *Midwest Quarterly* and *Beautiful Obstacles*. Both books were finalists for the Oregon Book Award. She teaches full time at Clackamas Community College.

**Robin Reynolds Barre** lives on Whidbey Island where she writes, teaches, and is presently working towards her master's degree in depth psychology. She is especially passionate about art journaling and the expressive arts.

**Ivon B. Blum** is a retired L.A. lawyer and the author of *River of Souls: A Novel of the American Myth* (www.riverofsouls.com), several short stories and poems. He is a member of Western Writers of America and Cambria Writers' Workshop. His story, "Fishstalker," was first published in *Flyfishing News*.

**Erv Bobo** is past Contributing Editor to *Computer Monthly* and *Computer Shopper* magazines. Retired near St. Louis, Missouri, he has published hundreds of computer articles and about 15 short stories for magazines such as *Adam, Knight, Spree, Hi-Life, Gent*. Of twelve short stories published in *Far West* magazine, two were nominated for the Western Writers of America Spur Award.

**Larry Bullis** has been a photographer in the Northwest for forty years, working n ine art and editorial media. He teaches photography at Skagit Valley College and Tacoma Community College.

**Patricia Brodie** is a clinical social worker with a private psychotherapy practice in Concord, MA. She has a Master's degree in English Literature from Boston College and has had poems accepted for publication in *Potpourri, Poetry Motel, The Raintown Review, Edge City Review, California Quarterly,* and *Colere.*

**Helen L. Campbell** is author of a published novel and two books of poetry. Her articles, poems, and short stories have appeared in *Grit, Scholastic Scope, Grade Teacher, Jack and Jill, Catholic Digest* and *Highlights for Children.* In 2001, she received the Idaho Writers' League Writer of the Year award.

**Christin Chaya** taught Special Education, then established a practice in depth-oriented psychotherapy. Following a serious car accident, resulting in brain and spinal damage, Christin was unable to continue her work. She then focused on her own recovery using singing, writing, and artwork as avenues for healing and creating a new life.

**Elizabeth Engstrom** is the author of nine books, over 200 short stories, articles and essays, and editor of four anthologies. Her most recent titles are *Black Leather, Suspicions, Lizard Wine,* and *Lizzie Borden.* She is the Director of the Maui Writers Retreat and its Department of Continuing Education, and teaches fiction at writers conferences and seminars around the world. www.ElizabethEngstrom.com.

**Ann Gerike** is the author of *Old is Not Four-Letter Word* (Papier-Mache Press, 1997) and several published shorter pieces. A retired clinical psychologist now living on Whidbey Island, Washington, she is working on essays, short stories, a memoir, poetry, and a comic novel. Her children, grand-children, and sisters live too far away.

**Norton Girault's** poems and stories have appeared in publications such as *MSS, Crescent Review, Timbuktu,* and *Snake Nation Review.* A Norfolk, VA resident, he has been a scholar at Bread Loaf Writers' Conference and a guest at Yaddo and MacDowell writers' colonies. "Goya's Monsters" won honorable mention in the 72nd Irene Leache Literary Contest and was published in that contest's publication.

**Sharon Goldner's** work has appeared in issues of *The Baltimore Review, Wordwrights Magazine,* and in *Kitchen Sink Press Anthologies.* She has received several awards for her work and a recent nomination for the Pushcart Prize. But most importantly, Sharon wants everyone to know she's having a good hair day.

**Rebecca Goodrich** lived in Sitka, Alaska for sixteen years before migrating south to warmer and dryer climes. She now resides in Moscow, Idaho where she is completing a Master of Fine Arts degree in Creative Writing from the University of Idaho. "Crossing Cold Water: Voyages to the Last Frontier" appeared in the Spring/Summer 2002 issue of *Potomac Review* (issue 33).

**Antoinette Grove** is a Northwest native living with her husband and two daughters on Whidbey Island, Washington where she has achieved an uneasy truce with the deer, rabbits and slugs but continues to battle blackberry bushes for supremacy of the world. Her writing credits include a dozen short stories in both national and regional markets as well as humor, business profiles and poetry.

**Donald Hall** has published fifteen books of poems, most recently *The Painted Bed,* which Houghton Mifflin published in April of 2002. His other books of poems include *Without, The Old Life, The Museum of Clear Ideas, Old and New Poems,* and *The One Day*. His poetry has won the National Book Critics Circle Award, the Los Angeles Times Book Award, and he has been three times nominated for the National Book Award. In 2003, Houghton Mifflin will publish his new and selected short stories, *Willow Temple*.

**Christopher Howell's** seventh collection of poems, *Just Waking*, was released this Fall by Lost Horse Press. He has been recipient of two fellowships from the National Endowment for the Arts, and three Pushcart Prizes; and his work has appeared in the pages of *Field, Gettysburg Review, Iowa Review, North American Review, Volt, Antioch Review, Hudson Review, Cutbank, Northwest Review, Poetry Northwest, Denver Quarterly, Colorado Review* and many other journals and anthologies. He teaches at Eastern Washington University's Inland NW Center for Writers, in Spokane, Washington.

**Ronald V. Hughes:** A boy from PA who married, worked in a factory, unmarried, went to VA, worked in a shipyard, married, then unmarried, got a BA & MA @ ODU, married, added a son, went to St. Lou, MO, teaches @ Comm. College, added a 2ndson, unmarried, in MFA @ UMSL, moving on, over and over...

**Manju Kak** is the author of *First Light in Colonelpura* (Penguin), *Requiem for an Unsung Revolutionary* (Ravi Dayal). Her research interests are rooted in aesthetics and communities particularly of the Kumaon Himalayas. One of them has been the Woodcarving Tradition. She lives in India where she is an activist on issues of governance and women's empowerment. She also paints. ww.manjukak.com

**JoAnn Kane** grew up in Minneapolis and spent the Kennedy years studying music and theater at the U of M. Her business/career thrives in music, her passion lies in writing, and her 21-year marriage to pianist/composer, Artie Kane, provides inspiration and encouragement for all her pursuits.

**Kristin King** earned an MFA from the University of Washington and lives in Seattle, where she is writing, teaching, and juggling. She won a Pushcart prize and has been published in *Calyx* and *Parting Gifts*. She has also won recognition from Writers at Work and the Utah Arts Council.

**Doug Knox** and his wife Marie live in Ashland, Ohio. They have three daughters, all attending college. Doug is a Christian freelance writer who writes fiction, creative nonfiction and Bible studies. He is working on his first novel.

**Kyle Kuhn** grew up in Iowa, where he attended the University of Northern Iowa. He is currently enrolled in the MFA program at Old Dominion University.

After leaving the stump ranch in North Idaho, **Rae Ellen Lee** worked as a secretary in the Foreign Service in D.C., Switzerland and Yugoslavia, and later as a landscape architect with the U.S. Forest Service. In 1997 she moved with her husband, Tom, to a sailboat in Bellingham to write. They now live on St. John in the U.S. Virgin Islands. She is currently writing a series of essays about her childhood on the stump ranch.

**Paul Lindholdt** is currently Assistant Professor of English at Eastern Washington University. He won an Academy of American Poets Award and has studied creative writing under Annie Dillard and American literature under Harrison Meserole. His chief research interest is environmental literature. Visit Paul Lindholdt's personal web site at: www.ewu.edu/cal/engl/plindholdt/home.html

**Marjiann Moss**, born in Central Washington, has traveled widely, collecting images and experiences to paint into word-pictures. Besides writing non-fiction, short fiction, lyrics and music, she has performed her poetry throughout the Northwest, including on public radio. Her play "Moira's Song" won the 1998 Puget Sound New Plays Project. "Firewood" received Fourth Place in the Whidbey Island Writers' community writing competition in 2002.

**Duane Niatum** has achieved international recognition as editor of two widely read and best-known anthologies of Native American poetry and as author of several volumes of his own award-winning poetry. He has also published essays and short stories that have been translated into more than 12 languages, and was invited in June of 1983 to attend the International Poetry Festival in Rotterdam. "With a Little Help from Raven" was published in *Archae*.

**Nnedi Okorafor** is a writer from Chicago. Her novel, *Zahrah the Windseeker*, is scheduled for release from Houghton Mifflin in early 2004. Okorafor's short story, "the Winds of Harmattan," will be published in *Mojo Conjure Stories*, edited by Nalo Hopkinson (Warner Aspect). www2.uic.edu/~nokora1

**Renée Olander's** poems have appeared in journals and anthologies, including *HEArt - human equity through art*, *13th Moon, Verse & Universe, Amelia, Sistersong-Women Across Cultures*, and others. With Luisa Igloria, she edited *Turnings: Writing on Women's Transformations*, published by the Friends of Women's Studies at Old Dominion U. "Song for a Ghost of Lake Drummond" was published in the chapbook *Wild Flights*.

**Natalie Olsen** is a Whidbey Island, Washington fiber artist whose writing has appeared in *Inksplash, Signals, The Seattle Times, Eastsideweek*, the 1999 King County Poetry & Art on Buses Project and The Cancer Poetry Project: Poems by Cancer Patients and Those Who Love Them. "New Roads" appeared in paint me a poem: a canvas of words, published as part of the 1999 Poetry & Art on the Buses Project.

**Jay Paul**, who lives with his wife and their gardens in Virginia, recently returned to lifting weights, being too old not to. His book, *Going Home in Flood Time* (poems from The *Christian Century, Poetry Northwest, Shenandoah,* and others) appeared from Ink Drop Press in 1999.

**Philip Raisor** has published nonfiction, poetry, fiction, and interviews in *The Southern Review, Poetry Northwest, Midwest Quarterly, Contemporary Literature,* and elsewhere. His edited collection of essays, *Tuned and Under Tension: The Recent Poetry of W. D. Snodgrass,* was published by the University of Delaware Press in 1999.

**Dorothy Read** started her writing career as a journalist, but abandoned social news and humor columns for teaching in 1968. Recently retired, she devotes her time to writing and encouraging other writers. She has work published in *Take Our Words for Whidbey,* an anthology home-based on Whidbey Island in Washington.

**Liam Rector's** books of poems are *American Prodigal* and *The Sorrow of Architecture.* He edited *The Day I Was Older: On the Poetry of Donald Hall,* and with Tree Swenson he recently co-edited *Fastening the Voice to the Page: On the Poetry of Frank Bidart.* He directs the graduate Writing Seminars at Bennington College and lives in Manhattan. "Back to Country with Pulitzer" was originally published in *American Poetry Review.*

**Susan Rich,** author of *The Cartographer's Tongue Poems of the World,* recently won the PEN West Poetry award and the Peace Corps Writers award. Her poems have appeared in many journals including the *Bellingham Review, Christian Science Monitor, DoubleTake,* and *Many Mountains Moving.* She teaches in the Antioch University-LA MFA program and at Highline Community College.

**Patrick Riley** spent 17 years writing nonfiction and marketing materials for high technology companies. His fiction and non-fiction have been widely published. He is currently working on a novel and is a member of the Mystery Writers of America. "The Icehouse" originally appeared in the February 2001 issue of the literary journal, *The Virginia Adversaria*.

**Richard Robbins'** collection of poems *Famous Persons We Have Known* was published by Eastern Washington University Press in 2000. He currently lives in Mankato, MN, with his wife, the poet Candace Black. The poem, "Fin de Siècle Sonnet out of Town," first appeared in *Visions-International*.

**Pattiann Rogers** has published ten books of poetry. The most recent, *Song of the World Becoming, New and Collected Poems*, 1981—2001 (Milkweed Editions), was a finalist for the LA Times Book Award and an Editor's Choice, Top of the List, in Booklist. Rogers has received two NEA Grants, a Guggenheim Fellowship, and a Lannan Poetry Fellowship. Her poem, "Watching the Ancestral Prayers of Vernerable Others," was included in her book, *Song of the World Becoming, New and Collected Poems*.

**Maureen McGregor Scully** lives at the base of Mount Rainier. She has an MFA from Goddard College, Vermont. Her work has appeared in *PawPrints*, *Expressions*, *The Circle Magaine*, *Bad HairCut*, and *Beyond Parallax*. She recently finished her first novel *Barn Dogs*, and is happily at work on a second novel. "Spade" was published in *Beyond Parallax*, The Literary and Visual Arts Journal of Centralia College, 1997.

**Eva Shaw, Ph.D.**, of Carlsbad, California, is the prolific writer of more than 1000 articles and 60 books, many award-winning titles. She teaches writing online at 800 colleges and universities through Education To Go. An expert on gardening as therapy and recovery, she speaks nationally on this topic. Her essay, *Gardening with a Pen*, was originally published in part in www.simplejoy.com.

Originally from Washington's Yakima Valley, **Victory Lee Schouten** has made her home on Whidbey Island for the past thirteen years. Victory's first book, *Wolf Love*, was published in 2000, the paperback is due out in 2003. She is a board member of the Washington Poets Association. More of her poetry can be seen at www.greatpath.com

**Maurya Simon** has published five volumes of poetry, including, *The Golden Labyrinth* (University of Missouri Press, 1995) and the recent limited edition, letter-press book, *A Brief History of Punctuation*. She received a 1999-2000 Fellowship in Poetry from the National Endowment for the Arts; she was a Visiting Artist in June 2002 at the American Academy in Rome. Simon teaches Creative Writing at the University of California, Riverside and lives in the Angeles National Forest in Southern California.

**Wayne Ude** is author of stories that have appeared in *Ploughshares, North American Review, Greenfield Review, Scree, Aspen Anthology,* and *The Last Good Place*. His books include *Becoming Coyote; Maybe I Will Do Something: Seven Tales of Coyote,* for ages 10 and up; and *Buffalo and Other Stories*. Since 1993 he has lived, written, and sometimes taught on Whidbey Island, Washington.

**Chika Unigwe** is currently a PhD student at the University of Leiden, Holland, writing a dissertation on Igbo Women's Literature. Her works include a collection of poetry, *Tear Drops* (1993), " Touched by an Angel," a short story broadcast on the BBC World Service (1998) and poetry and stories in various journals. She is married to Jan Karel Vandenhoudt and is a mother to three boys.

**Barbara Whitby**, originally from England, has spent most of her life in Nova Scotia. Now retired, she is full-time author, film 'extra', novice crew person, belly dancer and ardent traveler. She recently rode an elephant in the jungles of Sri Lanka and lived to broadcast her experience on CBC Radio. Her essay, "Voyage of Discovery," was originally published in *We Belong to the Sea*, a Nova Scotia Anthology, ed. Meddy Stanton.

**Rowena Williamson** has lived in Coupeville, Washington for 11 years with her husband Phil. In 2000 she won the Stella Cameron Prize for her adult novel and third prize for her young adult novel at the Pacific Northwest Writers Conference. She is a member of Whidbey Writers Group, and her work appears in their latest edition.

**Andrena Zawinski**, raised in Pittsburgh, PA, teaches in Oakland, CA. She is a San Francisco Bay Area coordinator for Poets for Peace as well as Feature Editor at PoetryMagazine.com. Her collection, *Traveling in Reflected Light*, is from Pig Iron Press; her latest chapbook is *Greatest Hits 1991-2001* from Pudding House. "The Narrative Thread" appeared in the *Haight Ashbury Literary Journal* and received a first prize from the San Francisco Bay Area Poets Coalition 2002 competition.

**Susan Zwinger** completed her Masters at the Writers' Workshop at the University of Iowa and a doctorate from Penn. State. Her books include *The Last Wild Edge* and *Stalking the Ice Dragon* (recipient of the Governor's Authors Award in 1992), *Still Wild, Always Wild*, and, co-authored with her mother, Ann Haymond Zwinger, *Women In Wilderness*. Susan teaches many workshops and classes in different locations such as North Cascades Institute.

The Whidbey Island Writers Association reaches out to writers around the globe with this anthology, with our e-mail ewsletter highlighting writing tips and markets, and with a nationally-acclaimed annual conference that showcases presenters, agents and editors so attendees can network and learn within an uplifting and enriching environment. A non-profit organization, we offfer options for college credits and youth scholarships to the Whidbey Island Writers Conference. Sponsoring year-round seminars, classes, readings, signing oportunities and promotional services, our mission as writers serving writers impacts the lives of many.

For more information:

Whibey Island Writers Association
Celeste Mergens, Director
P.O. Box 1289
Langley, WA 98260
email: writers@whidbey.com
www.whidbey.com/writers